The Stewart English Program

Book 2
Grammar Plus . . .

Donald S. Stewart

About the author: Donald S. Stewart taught English at Belmont Hill School, an independent school for boys in Belmont, Massachusetts. In 1990 he founded Write for College, an intensive summer writing course that he directed for 25 years, preparing high school students from the Boston area for the writing challenges of college and beyond. In 2015 he took the course online at http://writingwhatever.com.

Published by BookLocker.com, Inc., St. Petersburg, Florida.

Printed on acid-free paper.

BookLocker.com, Inc.
2018

Second edition

Cover designed by Shar www.fiverr.com/landofawes

CONTENTS

INTRODUCTION

I have always been intrigued by the question put to me years ago by a colleague, a biology teacher. "What animals," he asked, "were the last to learn about the ocean?" After I quickly gave up, he explained that birds knew about the ocean because they had seen it from the air. The creatures dwelling on land knew about it because they had walked along the shore. But because they were immersed in it, living in it and breathing it, the animals that learned last about the sea that surrounded them, that touched them every moment of their lives, were the fish.

We are like those fish, and the sea we swim in is our English language. We are born into it, frolic in it, occasionally get lost in it, and grow in it. And finally there comes the time when we begin to learn about it. We learn the names of the parts, how those parts work together, and how to make them work for us. That is why this series is called *Principles Plus*, *Grammar Plus*, and *Writing Plus*.

The major premise of this book is that the study of grammar *can* lead to better writing—and better reading and speaking. And so can the study of punctuation. But they must all be learned together, in a logical sequence, with each new piece building upon the lessons that came before. That is why virtually all exercises in these books call for written responses. The physical act of writing, whether it be an apt comparison, a phrase that captures the look on a character's face, or a clause that cements a logical relationship between ideas, contributes far more to both the pleasure and the effectiveness of the lesson than does the mere identification of a grammatical puzzler. Except for a handful of exercises, there is no single right answer, but instead an opportunity for the student to demonstrate both understanding of the lesson and creativity.

I wish to express my indebtedness to the late Francis Christensen and his wife, Bonniejean, for the inspiration for these textbooks. *Writing Plus*, the third in the series, is my revision of their masterpiece, *The Christensen Rhetoric Program*, which proved beyond a doubt that writing can be taught actively, not just reactively. Their method, of observation, discovery, and assimilation is the most natural of learning styles for the young people who stand at the threshold of opportunity and responsibility as the writers of the future.

May I also thank the many students I taught at Belmont Hill School over the years, for their encouragement, their enthusiasm in collecting the sample sentences from their favorite books, and their willingness to be the most honest of critics as I refined my presentation. The sparkle in their eyes has been my greatest reward.

Donald S. Stewart

1. VERBS

To express a complete thought, you need a subject and a verb.
The verb might express an action performed by the subject:

| She *erased* the blackboard carefully. |
| The children *are building* a snow fort. |
| We *slept* until noon. |
| My mother *will be working* all day tomorrow. |

Or, the verb might show only that something exists, or is in a certain condition:

| My favorite artist *is* Picasso. |
| His answer *was* wrong. |
| We *became* nervous. |

TYPES OF VERBS

There are three types of verbs that you should know.

1. **Transitive:** A transitive verb shows action and is followed by a direct object.

    | We *discovered* a hidden *treasure*. |
    | My aunt *sent* me a *birthday card*. |
    | Someone *has borrowed* my *cleats*. |

2. **Intransitive:** An intransitive verb also shows action but is not followed by a direct object.

    | The cat *purred*. |
    | My hat *fell* into the water. |
    | Mount Vesuvius *has* not *erupted* recently. |

3. **Linking:** A linking verb is not followed by a direct object, but it is followed by a predicate nominative (a noun, or a pronoun in the nominative case—See p. 80) or a predicate adjective. A predicate nominative or a predicate adjective is sometimes called a **subject complement**, because it completes what the verb has said about the subject.

    | David *is* my best *friend*. |
    | I knew the winner *would be he* who had the best pit crew. |
    | They *grew restless* listening to the long speech. |

    Forms of *to be:*

    | *is* | *am* | *are* | |
    | *was* | *were* | *will be* | |
    | *shall be* | *could be* | *should be* | *might have been* |

Verbs of the senses:	*look*	*feel*	*sound*	*taste*	*smell*

Other linking verbs:	*appear*	*seem*	*become*	*remain*
	grow	*turn*	*prove*	

Linking verb followed by predicate noun:

David *is* our new *neighbor*.

She *must be* a *teacher*.

You *should have been* a *football player*.

He *became* a *minister* at the age of fifty-three.

Linking verb followed by pronoun in the nominative case (after forms of *to be*):

Was it *she* who called last night?

The real thieves *were they* whom they had hired to guard the money.

Linking verb followed by adjective:

The milk *tasted sour*.

You *seem unhappy*.

I *feel bad* that I can't come to your party.

Do not be confused by verbs that look the same but have different functions, depending on their meaning in the sentence:

He *smelled* the roses.	**transitive**		I *turned* the steering wheel.	**transitive**
The roses *smelled* lovely.	**linking**		I *turned* red.	**linking**
			I *turned* into the driveway.	**intransitive**

To prepare for the first two exercises, study the simple sentences below and review the basics:

- Transitive takes a direct object.
- Intransitive doesn't.
- Linking takes a predicate noun, a predicate adjective, or a pronoun, nominative case.

Transitive	Intransitive	Linking
I *bought* an ice cream.	He *went* home.	They *remained* quiet.
Rita *erased* her answer.	Dad *sneezed* loudly.	The information *proved* false.
They *knew* how to type.	We *applauded* politely.	He *became* my favorite actor.
I *am trying* to fix the lamp.	I *will be sitting* nearby.	Everyone *must have been* happy.
She *will inherit* a fortune.	You *might be elected*.	*Could* the caller *have been* she?

VERBS

EXERCISE A: types of verbs   Accuracy _____ Creativity _____

Directions: Use the following verbs to create interesting sentences. Make sure that you are using them correctly, as transitive, intransitive, or linking verbs. Also make sure that you are using them as main verbs. Notice that you will be graded on both accuracy and creativity.

Example:	(*write*) as a transitive verb	
Incorrect:	I want to write a poem about my cat.	(*want* is the main verb)
Incorrect:	I tried writing a poem about my cat.	(*tried* is the main verb)
Incorrect:	I have written on both sides of the paper.	(*have written* is intransitive)
Correct:	I *have written* a poem about my cat.	(*have written* is transitive)

TRANSITIVE VERBS

1. (*locate*) _____

   _____

2 (*dig*)_____

   _____

3. (*write*) _____

   _____

4. (*return*)_____

   _____

5. (*maneuver*)_____

   _____

6. (*produce*)_____

   _____

7. (*buy*)_____

   _____

INTRANSITIVE VERBS

8. (*run*)_____

   _____

9. (*sing*) _____

    _____

10. (*battle*) _____

    _____

11. (*swim*) _____

    _____

12. (*remain*) _____

    _____

13. (*hide*) _____

    _____

LINKING VERBS

14. (*remain*+ predicate noun) _____

    _____

15. (*look*+ predicate adjective) _____

    _____

16. (*be*+ predicate noun) _____

    _____

17. (*become*+ predicate noun) _____

    _____

18. (*taste*+ predicate adjective) _____

    _____

19. (*be*+ pronoun in nominative case) _____

    _____

20. (*be*+ predicate adjective) _____

    _____

VERBS

Name: _____

EXERCISE B: subject complements

Accuracy _____ Creativity _____

Directions: This exercise illustrates the use of subject complements. Fill in the blanks with your own creations as directed. Notice that you will be graded on both accuracy and creativity.

1. _____
        (proper noun + form of **to be** *+ predicate noun)*

    _____ if _____
                                        (finish the sentence)

    _____ .

2. Most _____
              (plural noun + linking verb other than **to be***)*

    _____ when _____
    (predicate adjective)   *(finish the sentence)*

    _____ .

3. Tom's new_____
              (noun + any linking verb)

    _____ than he expected.
    (predicate adjective)

4. _____ tastes as _____ as
                (noun)   *(predicate adjective)*

    _____ .
    (finish the sentence)

5. My _____ could never have been a
          (noun)

    _____ , because _____
        (predicate noun)   *(finish the sentence)*

    _____ .

6. As soon as _____ ,
                        (finish the idea)

    my brother became _____ .
                          (predicate noun or adjective)

7. _____ grew more _____
           (pronoun)   *(predicate adjective)*

   as _____
              (finish the sentence)

   _____ .

8. My mother _____ happy when I _____
         *(linking verb other than **to be**)*   *(finish the sentence)*

   _____ .

9. The _____ will be _____
                  (noun)   *(pronoun, nominative case)*

   who _____ .
             (finish the sentence)

10. The _____ who _____
                   (noun)   *(finish the idea)*

    _____ could not have been _____ .
                                                            (pronoun, nominative case)

PRINCIPAL PARTS OF THE VERB

There are four principal parts of a verb.

1. **Infinitive:** This is the form we get when we put *to* in front of the verb.

   Examples: *to type*   *to change*   *to receive*   *to find*   *to go*   *to be*

   The infinitive form of the verb, using the *to*, will never itself be the main verb of a sentence. Rather, it is the form we use to create the present tense.

   Examples: I *type*   we *change*   you *receive*   you *find*   they *go*

   The third person present tense usually just adds *-s* or *-es* to the infinitive.

   Examples: he *types*   she *changes*   it *receives*   she *finds*   he *goes*

   The verb *to be* is an important exception to these rules:

	Singular	**Plural**
First person	I *am*	we *are*
Second person	you *are*	you *are*
Third person	he, she, it *is*	they *are*

   We will see in later chapters that the infinitive form of the verb, using the *to*, may be used as a noun, an adjective, or an adverb. That is why it is important to know this form of the verb.

2. **Past:** Regular verbs form the past tense by adding *-ed* or *-d* to the infinitive.

   Examples: *looked*   *shattered*   *walked*   *dated*

   Irregular verbs form the past tense in a variety of ways.

   Examples: *find/found*   *break/broke*   *go/went*   *cast/cast*   *be/was, were*

3. **Past participle:** Regular verbs form the past participle by adding *-ed* or *-d* to the infinitive, the same as the past tense. Notice that they often have a form of *have* right before them.

   Examples: have *locked*   had *shattered*   has *walked*   have *dated*

   Irregular verbs form the past participle in a variety of ways.

   Examples: have *found*   have *broken*   had *gone*   has *cast*   had *been*

4. **Present participle:** This form is made by adding *-ing* to the infinitive.

   Examples: *finding*   *going*   *wearing*   *remembering*   *being*

   Spelling alert: Notice the occasional addition, deletion, or change of letters.

   Examples: *type/typing*   *begin/beginning*   *die/dying*

USING THE DICTIONARY

When you look up a verb in the dictionary, you will see the word, then a guide to pronunciation, and then the letters *v., v. t.,* or *v. i.* The letter *v* stands for *verb*, the letter *t* stands for *transitive*, and the letter *i* stands for *intransitive*.

You will also see the principal parts of the verb. The infinitive form is used to list the verb in the dictionary. With a regular verb, you will then see the past and the past participle (it is listed only once, since the two forms are the same), and the present participle. With an irregular verb, you will see the past and the past participle listed separately, and the present participle form.

	Infinitive	Past	Past participle	Present participle
Regular verbs	move	moved	moved	moving
	cook	cooked	cooked	cooking
	waddle	waddled	waddled	waddling
Irregular verbs	go	went	gone	going
	break	broke	broken	breaking
	cast	cast	cast	casting

TENSES OF THE VERB

There are three simple tenses, **present**, **past**, and **future**. Within each of those time slots there may be an action that is still in progress (the present, past, or future **progressive**) or that has recently been finished or "perfected" (the present, past, or future **perfect**). Or, some of the action has been finished but some continues (the present, past, or future **perfect progressive**). The following examples illustrate these tenses.

	Simple	Progressive	Perfect	Perfect Progressive
Present	I find	I am finding	I have found	I have been finding
Past	I found	I was finding	I had found	I had been finding
Future	I will find	I will be finding	I will have found	I will have been finding

So, in which tenses is the present participle of *to find* used? _____

And the past participle of *to find*? _____

And the past participle of *to be*? _____

VERBS

EXERCISE C: principal parts of verbs

Directions: Look up the following verbs in a dictionary and find their principal parts. Fill in the blanks with those correct forms. Notice that some have more than one possible form. You will be graded only on accuracy.

Infinitive	Past	Past Participle	Present Participle
be			
bear			
burst			
choose			
dive			
fly			
have			
lay			
lead			
lend			
lie (recline)			
lie (speak falsely)			
rise			
set			
shine			
shrink			
sink			
sit			
swim			
swing			

VERBS

Name: _____

EXERCISE D: tenses of verbs

Accuracy _____

Directions: Using the principal parts from Exercise C, fill in the blanks below with the indicated tenses of the given verbs.

Simple present

It _____
(be)

She _____
(choose)

You _____
(sit)

Simple past

She _____
(burst)

Everyone _____
(have)

He _____
(lead)

Simple future

They_____
(be)

We _____
(choose)

I _____
(rise)

Present progressive

We_____
(bear)

They _____
(lie–recline)

It _____
(sit)

Past progressive

Few _____
(be)

He _____
(have)

They _____
(lead)

Future progressive

You_____
(fly)

Both _____
(lay)

I _____
(lie–recline)

Present perfect

You _____
(be)

He _____
(bear)

I _____
(lie–recline)

Past perfect

We _____
(fly)

It _____
(have)

Several _____
(lie–speak falsely)

Future perfect

It_____
(burst)

I _____
(lay)

Many _____
(shrink)

Present perfect progressive

We _____
(have)

The hen _____
(lay)

She _____
(lie–speak falsely)

Past perfect progressive

They _____
(bear)

We _____
(lie–recline)

It _____
(rise)

Future perfect progressive

Many_____
(choose)

Few _____
(fly)

Both _____
(have)

VERBS

Name: _____

EXERCISE E: verb tenses in writing   Accuracy _____ Creativity _____

Directions: Write a sentence for each verb given, using it as the **main verb** of the sentence, in the indicated tense. Notice that you will be graded on both accuracy and creativity.

1. (*be*) (**present progressive**)_____

   _____

2. (*burst*) (**past progressive**)_____

   _____

3. (*sit*) (**future progressive**)_____

   _____

4. (*lie–speak falsely*) (**present perfect progressive**)_____

   _____

5. (*fly*) (**past perfect progressive**)_____

   _____

6. (*rise*) (**past**)_____

   _____

7. (*set*) (**past**)_____

   _____

8. (*have*) (**past perfect**)_____

   _____

9. (*lead*) (**past**)_____

   _____

10. (*choose*) (**future perfect**)_____

    _____

11. (*lie–recline*) (**past perfect**)_____

_____

12. (*lay*) (**future perfect progressive**)_____

_____

13. (*shrink*) (**past perfect**)_____

_____

14. (*bear*) (**past perfect**)_____

_____

15. (*swim*) (**future perfect**)_____

_____

16. (*dive*) (**past**)_____

_____

17. (*swing*) (**future perfect progressive**)_____

_____

18. (*sink*) (**past perfect**)_____

_____

19. (*lend*) (**past**)_____

_____

20. (*shine*) (**present perfect**)_____

_____

HELPING VERBS

In the three exercises you have done so far, you have been writing sentences that have explored the various principal parts of verbs. In order to write those sentences, you had to use other verbs to get the main verb into the tense that you wanted. Here are the five kinds of **helping verbs**.

Forms of *to be*	am	is	are	was	were	be	been	being	
Forms of *to do*	do	does	did						
Forms of *to have*	has	have	had						
Modals	could	would	should	will	might	may	must	shall	can
Helping phrases	has to	have to	had to	used to	(be) going to	ought to			

Helping verbs may be used with any principal part of a verb except the past tense. A main verb may have up to four helping verbs to put it into a particular tense. Here is how the helping verbs may be used with the verb *to take*, using the subject *They*. Try substituting the other helpers to see all the possibilities. Also, when you study charts like this, read them vertically as well as horizontally.

take	taking	taken
They *take*.	They *are taking*. They *have been taking*.	They *are taken*. They *are being taken*. They *have taken*. They *have been taken*.
They *do take*.		
They *could take*.	They *could be taking*. They *could have been taking*.	They *could have taken*. They *could have been taken*. They *could be taken*. They *could have been being taken*. (rare)
They *used to take*.	They *used to be taking*.	They *used to be taken*.

VERB ISSUES

Eternal truths: An eternal truth is a fact or idea that was, is, and always will be true. Even though the main verb of the sentence might be in the past tense, express the eternal truth in the present tense.

> He knew that honesty *is* the best policy, but he continued to lie.
> Benjamin Franklin demonstrated that lightning *is* electricity.

Voice: A sentence is in the **active voice** when the subject is doing the action of the verb. A sentence is in the **passive voice** when the action of the verb is being done to the subject.

All the verbs in the Tenses of the Verb chart on page 8 were in the active voice. The passive voice is constructed by using the past participle form of the verb, along with a form of *to be*, and sometimes one or more other helpers. Notice that the sentence you just read was in the passive voice.

The passive voice is useful when we don't know or don't want to say who or what did the verb.

> It *was reported* that...
> The window *must have been broken* when...

For most writing, though, you should write in the active voice for the most clarity and vitality.

Mood: There are three moods of the verb in English.

The **indicative** mood is the most common, as these verbs indicate what is happening in the world around us. That is the kind we have been studying so far.

The **imperative** mood is used to express a request or a command. It is simply the infinitive form of the verb, without *to*.

Watch me blow a bubble.
Give me a hand.
Take off your hat.
Be here on time.

The **subjunctive** mood is used to express a situation or condition contrary to fact, or to express a wish or a hypothesis. There are two ways to form the subjunctive. Sometimes we use the infinitive form of the verb instead of the usual indicative form.

I asked that *I be* allowed to speak first.	(not *I am*)
The doctor recommended that *she go* on a vacation.	(not *she goes*)

The other way to form the subjunctive is to change the verb *was* to *were*. This is usually done in a clause beginning with *as*, *as if*, or *as though*, or in a wish.

He yelled as if *he were* being murdered.	(not *he was*)
I wish *I were* ten years younger.	(not *I was*)

Be cautious with the subjunctive. Remember that these situations are contrary to fact, theoretical, imaginary. He was not being murdered. I am not ten years younger.

However, sometimes you are dealing with a situation that might be true. The subjunctive mood is inappropriate in these cases.

It looks as if *he is* going to lose.	(he probably will)
If *she was* here, she left no trace behind.	(maybe she was)

Sequence: The **perfect tenses** and the **perfect progressive tenses** deserve special attention.

When you are referring to two events, and one precedes the other, you must express the time sequence properly. Use the perfect or the perfect progressive tense for the earlier event.

Incorrect:	If I *did* my homework, I would not have failed.
Correct:	If I *had done* my homework, I would not have failed.
Incorrect:	I *waited* two hours before you arrived.
Correct:	I *had waited* two hours before you arrived.
Correct:	I *had been waiting* two hours before you arrived.
Incorrect:	She told the doctor she *had* the problem for over a year.
Correct:	She told the doctor she *had had* the problem for over a year.
Correct:	She told the doctor she *had been having* the problem for over a year.
Incorrect:	She will tell the doctor she *had* the problem for over a year.
Correct:	She will tell the doctor she *has had* the problem for over a year.
Correct:	She will tell the doctor she *has been having* the problem for over a year.

VERBS

EXERCISE F: verbs and their helpers   Accuracy _____ Creativity _____

Name: _____

Directions: Fill in the blanks below with verbs as labeled.

1. My little brother _____ sick on the merry-go-round.
    (linking verb)

2. I _____ an honor student if I had just tried a
    *(helper + helper + linking verb, not **to be**)*

    little harder.

3. His priceless Rembrandt painting _____ last night.
    (helper + past participle)

4. By the time I learn all my lines for the audition, the cast members for the play _____ already
    (helper)

    _____ .
    (helper + helper + past participle)

5. _____ he _____ the magnitude of the problem?
    (helper)   *(transitive verb)*

6. The teachers _____ every morning at ten o'clock.
    (intransitive verb)

7. This morning the three golden retrievers _____ in the back yard.
    (intransitive verb)

8. "The prisoner _____ not _____
    (helper)   *(helper + helper + present participle)*

    on the night of the crime," the lawyer explained.

9. When we arrived at the scene of the accident, the driver _____ hardly _____ .
    (helper)   *(present participle)*

10. Tomorrow we _____ if we are lucky.
    (helper + helper + past participle)

11. _____ everyone _____ in the geometry course?
    (helper)   *(present participle)*

12. I knew by the voice that it _____ she.
    (helper + helper + linking verb)

13. Without your help, we never _____ him.
    (helper + helper + past participle)

14. The finalists _____ they who have won at least seven games.
    (helper + linking verb)

15. It _____ always _____ that way.
    (helper)   *(helper + past participle)*

16. From now on, it _____ always _____ this way.
    (helper)   *(helper + past participle)*

17. The finished product _____ better than I had expected.
    *(linking verb, not **to be**)*

18. Last Saturday three of my friends _____ until I _____
    (intransitive verb)   *(helper)*

    _____ them to leave.
    (transitive verb)

19. My boss _____ nervous as the deadline approached.
    *(linking verb, not **to be**)*

20. My suggestion _____ by now.
    (helper + helper + helper + intransitive verb)

EXERCISE G: reading for verbs   Accuracy _____ Creativity _____

Directions: Now read in a good book, and pay attention to the verbs. Try to find verb phrases, those that are more than one word long. See if you can locate some verbs in the imperative or subjunctive mood—mysteries are good for that! Write just the simple subjects and the verb phrases in the spaces below, and tell the name of the book and the author.

Simple subject	Verb phrase

Title and Author: _____

2. NOUNS

A **noun** is the name of a person, a place, a thing, or an idea. A **common noun** is the name for a general member of a group. A **proper noun** is the name of a particular member of a group, and it is always capitalized.

COMMON NOUNS

person	child	uncle	friend	astronaut
place	city	yard	sky	diner
thing	desk	grass	horse	television
idea	truth	courage	wonder	imagination

PROPER NOUNS

person	Dr. Ann Bain	Mr. Holt	Betty	Captain Kirk
place	Saturn	Boston	Fiji	North America
thing	Nintendo	Eiffel Tower	Kia	Club Med
idea	Darwinism	Judaism	God	Romanticism

THE INFINITIVE PHRASE

The next type of noun is the **infinitive phrase**. You will recall from the chapter on verbs that the infinitive helps us create the present tense, the present participle, and the imperative and the subjunctive moods. But as a verb it never appeared with the word *to*.

As a noun, however, it usually does. We can use it as a simple infinitive or as an infinitive phrase in many of the same ways that a noun can be used.

subject	*To ski* is her favorite sport.
subject	*To start from the beginning* was necessary.
direct object	Neither of us wanted *to participate*.
direct object	I tried *to convince him to reconsider*.
object of preposition	The army would seek peace in any way except *to surrender*.
object of preposition	We had no choice but *to pack up and leave*.
subject complement	The worst thing he could do would be *to resign*.
subject complement	Her goal was *to get to the finish line alive*.
appositive	Their greatest desire, *to mountain climb,* finally came true.
appositive	Our decision, *to sell our house and go live in the woods*, brought us the peace we desired.

INFINITIVE PHRASE ISSUES

1. There are three interesting things to know about the infinitive phrase. First, the *to* may sometimes be omitted.

    We all saw you *[to] take* the answer sheet.
    I'll do anything but *[to] sing*.

2. Also, the infinitive may have its own subject, and if it is a pronoun, it is in the objective case.

    I invited *him to visit* us.
    My father helped *me [to] start* the car.
    We considered *her to be* the best candidate.

    See Chapter 7, "Pronouns," for a complete discussion of pronoun case.

3. And finally, as may be seen from three of the above examples, the infinitive may have its own direct object.

    I tried *to find my shoes* under the bed.

THE INFINITIVE PHRASE: SAMPLES

They began *to stir* though still the world outside the shelter was impossibly dangerous.
— William Golding, *Lord of the Flies*

Her habit was *to imagine the whole route before she actually moved herself to run.*
— Virginia Hamilton, *A White Romance*

Their business was *to toil, and to toil mightily, in the traces.*   — Jack London, *The Call of the Wild*

The trouble was, Colin didn't know whether he wanted *to join such an establishment.*
— J. Anthony Lukas, *Common Ground*

When she got Kicker, people told her the only way to get the wildness out of an ostrich was *to put him in an enclosure as near the house as possible while still young so that he could see people every day.*
—Dalene Matthee, *Fiela's Child*

I don't suppose it will knock any of you people off your perch *to read a contribution from an animal.*
— O. Henry, "Memoirs of a Yellow Dog"

She offered *to send someone over to pick up the check within the hour*, but I thought it was easier *to go ahead and put it on my card.*
—Sue Grafton, *J is for Judgment*

GERUNDS

In the same way that we took the infinitive form of the verb and used it as a noun, we can also take the present participle form and use it as a noun. Such a construction is called a **gerund phrase**.

Here are two examples of how the transformation from a verb phrase to a gerund phrase occurs.

Example #1	The runner was *sliding into home plate.*	**–*ing* verb form**
	sliding into home plate	**remove the phrase**
	Sliding into home plate proved to be a big mistake.	**subject**
	We practiced *sliding into home plate* for half an hour.	**direct object**
	Her specialty is *sliding into home plate.*	**subject complement**
	She won the game by *sliding into home plate.*	**object of the preposition**
	His trademark, *sliding into home plate*, made him the terror of the league.	**appositive**
Example #2	Mother was *stir-frying the chicken.*	**–*ing* verb form**
	stir-frying the chicken	**remove the phrase**
	Stir-frying the chicken was the fastest way to cook it.	**subject**
	My big sister loved *stir-frying the chicken.*	**direct object**
	His contribution to dinner was *stir-frying the chicken.*	**subject complement**
	After *stir-frying the chicken*, the chef piled it on top of the rice.	**object of the preposition**
	He delighted in his assignment, *stir-frying the chicken.*	**appositive**

A gerund may appear by itself or as part of a phrase, with a direct object, prepositional phrases, and other modifiers.

subject	*Writing* is a skill that needs constant practice.
subject	*Writing a journal during the summer* made Carolyn more observant.
direct object	I have not finished *eating.*
direct object	I have not finished *eating the cookies you baked for me last week.*
indirect object	His exam gave *cheating* a whole new meaning.
indirect object	She gave *staying on the balance beam* every ounce of her strength.
object of preposition	You must warm up before *playing.*
object of preposition	The rain did not interfere with *our having a good time.*
subject complement	Your first Trivia category is "*Gardening.*"
subject complement	My greatest thrill was *being chosen for the all-star team.*
appositive	I'm very proud of my hobby, *woodcarving.*
appositive	We had two choices, *warming the leftover hash* or *sending out for pizza.*

GERUND ISSUES

1. The possessive form of the noun or pronoun should be used before the gerund phrase to show to whom the action "belongs."

Did you enjoy *my singing* in the play?   *whose* singing?

Bill's arriving early upset his girlfriend.   *whose* arriving?

The teacher was distracted by the *boys' chattering* in the back row.   *whose* chattering?

2. Also, grammatical items in a series should all be of the same construction. Do not mix gerund phrases with other kinds of phrases or clauses.

Incorrect: I loved *your dancing and how you juggled* four bananas at once.

Correct: I loved your *dancing and juggling* four bananas at once.

Correct: I loved *how you danced and juggled* four bananas at once.

THE GERUND PHRASE: SAMPLES

In the act of *sounding the charge,* the captain found himself confronted by a wall of snapping flame.
—Janny Wurtz, *Master of White Storm*

When he had seen to the weather, Billy cleared each nostril by *holding its mate closed with his forefinger and blowing fiercely.*
—John Steinbeck, *The Red Pony*

Watching girls and devouring them with your eyes was something you did automatically.
—Robert Cormier, *The Chocolate War*

The night porter remembered *ringing up Miss Keene's room just after midnight and getting no reply.*
—Agatha Christie, *The Body in the Library*

The Colonel had spent most of his life in the Army, and so was very good at *telling everybody what that feller Hitler was going to do next, and putting his own interpretation on snippets of news that appeared in the daily papers relating to secret weapons and the movement of warships.*
—Rosamunde Pilcher, *The Shell Seekers*

Mother's swims consisted of *testing the water with the tip of a black bathing shoe, wading cautiously out to her knees, making some tentative dabs in the water with her hands, splashing a few drops on her shoulders, and* finally, in a moment of supreme courage, *pinching her nose and squatting down until the water reached her chest.*
—Frank B. Gilbreth, Jr., and Ernestine Gilbreth Carey, *Cheaper by the Dozen*

NOUNS

Name: _____

EXERCISE A: infinitive phrases

Accuracy _____ Creativity _____

Directions: In the spaces below, write infinitive phrases of your own creation. The function of the infinitive phrase is indicated beneath the line. Notice that you will be graded on both accuracy and creativity.

1. No one wanted _____ .
    (direct object)

2. _____
    (subject)

    _____ was the last thing we wanted to do.

3. The one project remaining is _____ .
    (subject complement)

4. _____
    (subject)

    _____ requires a full-time commitment.

5. When you buy this new car, there is no service required for the first 10,000 miles but _____
    *(object of the preposition **but**)*

    _____ .

6. Most of the seniors tried _____
    (direct object)

    _____ .

7. I know the first thing to do when fixing a leaky faucet— _____
    *(appositive without **to**)*

    _____ .

8. As a doctor his highest priority would be _____
    (subject complement)

    _____ .

9. _____ is _____ .
    (subject)   *(subject complement)*

10. We had three things to do before midnight: _____
    (appositive)

    _____ , _____
                                          (appositive)

    _____ , and _____ .
                      (appositive)

NOUNS

Name: _____

EXERCISE B: gerund phrases   Accuracy _____ Creativity _____

Directions: Fill in the spaces below with gerund phrases of your own creation. The function of the gerund phrase in the sentence is indicated beneath the line.

1. _____
   (subject)

   _____ proved to be our downfall.

2. _____ and _____
   (subject)   *(subject)*

   _____ is the only way to succeed.

3. We all tried _____ .
   (direct object)

4. _____ is not like
   (subject)

   _____ .
   (object of the preposition **like***)*

5. The mountain climber's main concern soon became _____ .
   (subject complement)

6. My summer activities, _____ and
   (appositive)

   _____ , were fun but didn't earn me any money.
   (appositive)

7. We can achieve our goal only by _____ ,
   (three objects of the preposition **by***)*

   _____ , and _____ .

8. At night school you have an opportunity to learn _____ ,
   (three objects of the infinitive **to learn***)*

   _____ , and _____ .

9. Both _____ and
   (subject)

   _____ were charged against the criminal.
   (subject)

10. After I finished building the bookcase, I had the choice of either _____
    (object of the preposition **of***)*

    _____ or _____ .
    (object of the preposition **of***)*

NOUN CLAUSES

Another kind of noun is called the **noun clause**. A clause is a group of words that contains a verb and a subject to go with it, and in later chapters you will learn about the adjective clause and the adverb clause.

A noun clause is most often used as the subject, the direct object, the subject complement, or the object of a preposition. There are three ways by which a sentence may become a noun clause.

1. You may add a subordinating conjunction to the beginning of a sentence. The most common subordinating conjunctions that introduce noun clauses are *that, the fact that, if,* and *whether*.

original sentence	We couldn't get the door closed.
add subordinator	*(The fact) that we couldn't get the door closed*
subject	*(The fact) that we couldn't get the door closed* made us nervous.
direct object	We suddenly realized *that we couldn't get the door closed.*
subject complement	Our biggest fear was *that we couldn't get the door closed.*
object of preposition	Nothing was wrong except *that we couldn't get the door closed.*

More examples:

The union leader declared *that the farm workers should be paid weekly rather than monthly.*

The fact that your mother didn't remind you is no excuse.

Your fascinating sister has nothing to do with *whether I'll come over for dinner.*

2. You may replace a noun or pronoun in a sentence with a **relative pronoun.** The relative pronouns to use are *who, whose, whom, which,* and *what,* and their *-ever* forms. Then move the relative pronoun to the beginning of the sentence, if necessary, and you may use the new construction as part of another sentence. Watch how the transformation occurs in the first example, then analyze how it happened in the others.

The singer was *Ella Fitzgerald*	
The singer was *who*	
... *who the singer was*	I finally remembered *who the singer was.*
These woods are *Mr. Appleseed's.*	I think I know *whose woods these are.*
I should invite *him.*	I asked my mother *whom I should invite.*
This month's magazine is missing.	Do you know *which is missing?*
We know *nothing.*	We are known by *what we know.*
Do you want *waffles or pancakes?*	You may have *whatever you want.*
Bill or Dave can start the job tomorrow.	*Whoever can start the job tomorrow* should be hired.

3. You may also replace an adverb in the original sentence with a relative adverb, *why, where, when,* or *how*. Then move the relative adverb to the beginning of the sentence, if necessary, and you have created a noun clause that can become part of another sentence. Watch how the transformation occurs in the first example, then analyze how it happens in the others.

They had left their bicycles *in the street.*
They had left their bicycles *where*

... *where they had left their bicycles*	They remembered *where they had left their bicycles.*

Yesterday she finished the report.	*When she finished the report* was not the issue.
You answered it *nervously.*	I knew you were lying by *how you answered the question.*

I wanted to go *because my cousin would be there.*	I finally told them *why I wanted to go.*

THE NOUN CLAUSE: SAMPLES

The boy knew *that his father was joking, that he would never take his friends away.*
—Robert Cormier, *I Am the Cheese*

What hit you first was the noise and the sweat.
—Virginia Hamilton, *A White Romance*

She did not know *what other money there was to be gained, or how, or on whom he spent it.*
—Nadine Gordimer, *July's People*

The trouble was, Colin didn't know *whether he wanted to join such an establishment.*
—J. Anthony Lukas, *Common Ground*

Once I asked Granny *what Uncle Busan did that was so bad,* but she wouldn't tell me.
—Olive Ann Burns, *Cold Sassy Tree*

After two days it became clear *that Tashi was deliberately hiding.*
—Alice Walker, *The Color Purple*

He knew *which doors stayed open,* and *which walls were thin,* and *which air vents carried sound.*
—John Grisham, *The Pelican Brief*

Whatever he had to do must be done today; tomorrow he would be incapable.
—Nevil Shute, *On the Beach*

It had never occurred to him *that one man could get the best of another by the simple expedient of telling him the truth.*
—Marjorie Kinnan Rawlings, *The Yearling*

Before noon the landlady put her head in and told Janice *that there was something for which she had to come downstairs.*
—Joanne Greenberg, *In This Sign*

From the way people treated her, it was clear *that they did not expect a great deal from Elizabeth.*
—Nancy Bond, *Another Shore*

NOUNS

Name: _____

EXERCISE C: noun clauses   Accuracy _____ Creativity _____

Directions: Fill in the blanks with noun clauses of your own creation. The function of the noun clause in the sentence is written beneath the line.

1. Mother finally discovered _____
    (direct object)

    _____ .

2. The fact that _____
    (subject)

    _____ made no difference to the security guard.

3. We knew nothing except _____
    *(object of the preposition **except**)*

    _____ .

4. Our first decision will be _____
    (subject complement)

    _____ .

5. _____
    (subject)

    _____ will decide the ultimate success of your endeavor.

6. Today or tomorrow, _____
    (appositive)

    _____ , will be fine with me.

7. Did you ever find out _____ ?
    (direct object)

8. _____ and
    (subject)

    _____ were still unclear.
    (subject)

9. The whole school will be affected by _____
    *(object of the preposition **by**)*

    _____ .

10. There were still two questions to be answered: _____
    (appositive)

    _____ and _____ ?
    (appositive)

EXERCISE D: reading for nouns   Accuracy _____

Directions: Now read in a good book and try to find a sentence that contains an infinitive phrase used as a noun, a sentence that contains a gerund phrase, and one that contains a noun clause. Write the complete sentences below, and put the phrase or clause in parentheses. Then tell how each is being used in the sentence. Also tell the title of the book and its author.

Infinitive phrase as noun: _____

_____

_____

Gerund phrase: _____

_____

_____

Noun clause: _____

_____

_____

Title and Author: _____

APPOSITIVES

An appositive is a noun or pronoun that restates another noun or pronoun (its *antecedent*) in the sentence.

> My favorite ice cream flavor, *chocolate*,...
> Our English teacher, *Mrs. Cheever*,...
> Her college major, *philosophy*, ...

Several times in this chapter you have been asked to write appositives, and you probably have done so with little difficulty. You saw that appositives don't have to be just single words. Any grammatical construction that acts as a noun may also be used as an appositive.

date	The year *1968* is often considered a turning point in American history.
pronoun	That's my friend's car, *the one spewing out black smoke*.
pronoun	We need a new chairman, *someone who is not afraid to make a decision*.
common nouns	Piles of trash were all over the back yard—*empty soda cans, paper plates, plastic cups, and even a few chicken bones*.
proper noun	Steinbeck's novel *The Grapes of Wrath* is on the summer reading list.
gerund phrase	The children looked forward to their Saturday ritual, *visiting their grandfather in the nursing home*.
	We have big plans for this weekend—*deep sea fishing on Saturday, camping overnight on Snake Island, and snorkeling on the reef on Sunday*.
infinitive phrase	Her one desire, *to swim in the Olympics*, finally came true.
noun clause	Any donation will be accepted, *whatever you can afford*.
noun clause	His excuse, *that the traffic was heavy and his car overheated*, sounded plausible.

Sometimes an appositive will appear elsewhere in the sentence. It may precede the noun or pronoun it refers to, or it may follow at some distance, as long as there is no other intervening word that might cause confusion.

> *A millionaire by the age of thirty*, Tom retired to a farm in Vermont.
> She quickly captured the imagination of the whole country, *a talented gymnast with a world-class smile*.

APPOSITIVE ISSUES

1. Be careful how you punctuate appositives. An appositive is set off from the rest of the sentence by commas if it is not absolutely necessary to make its antecedent clear. In the examples earlier, there is *one* favorite ice cream flavor, *one* English teacher, *one* college major, *one* desire, *one* ritual, *one* excuse. But if the appositive is "one of many," then it must not be set off by commas.

<u>Poe's story "The Tell-Tale Heart" kept me awake last night. **Poe wrote many stories.**</u>

<u>My brother, Sergio, is seven years old. **I have only the one brother.**</u>
My brother Sergio is seven years old. **I have more than one brother.**

2. If the appositive is a pronoun, it is in the same case as its antecedent.

<u>Two people, *Jean and she*, were selected. **nominative case, antecedent is subject**</u>
The director selected two people, *Jean and her*. **objective case, antecedent is object**

See Chapter 7, "Pronouns," for a complete discussion of pronoun case.

3. Sometimes an appositive is not exactly the same as its antecedent, but is a "subset" of it, just one of many items possible.

<u>I took one look at his face—the blood-shot *eyes*, the filthy *beard*, the toothless *grin*—and let out a scream.</u>

There is more to the face than just the eyes, the beard, and the grin, but these are the "subsets" the author wants you to notice. These are sometimes called noun phrases, but they behave the same way as appositives.

THE APPOSITIVE: SAMPLES

A cautious child, he would dip his toes in the swirling waters of life before taking a plunge.
—J. Anthony Lukas, *Common Ground*

On April 9, *the day King was buried in Atlanta*, White issued a statement.
—J. Anthony Lukas, *Common Ground*

Bonny had been Janine's best friend, *a friend so close* that even when the Darts moved to Colville, *an inner-city suburb*, they insisted on remaining friends, visiting each other after school, and spending weekends at one another's houses. —Margaret Mahy, *Memory*

On the birth of a second son, *my junior by seven years*, my parents gave up entirely their wandering life and fixed themselves in their native country. —Mary Shelley, *Frankenstein*

They walked on up the hill, and now a panorama started to unfold behind them, *a wide view over the flat plain to the sea at Port Phillip Bay ten miles away.* —Nevil Shute, *On the Beach*

I looked out my window and after a moment spotted him, *a noble, silent dog lying on a ledge above the entrance to a brownstone house in lower Fifth Avenue.*
—James Thurber, "The Admiral on the Wheel"

Mrs. Latoumelle, *the original founder, a motherly talkative lady with a cork leg and a past somehow relating to the theater*, had retired in 1805, *ten years previously*, to drink port and rest her cork leg on a sofa; but her place had been taken by her niece, *Mrs. Camperdowne*, of equally amiable and indulgent temperament. —Joan Aiken, *If I Were You*

NOUNS

Name: _____

EXERCISE E: appositives   Accuracy _____ Creativity _____

Directions: Fill in the blanks with appositives of your own creation. The antecedent is in **bold** type. Some blanks require specific grammatical constructions.

1. The **boy** who just moved in next door, _____

   _____ , has a pet iguana.

2. The two **cars**, _____

   _____ , collided at the intersection.

3. I finally had saved enough money to buy the one **thing** I had always wanted, _____

   _____ .

4. I can never spell the **word** _____ correctly.

5. My favorite summer **activity**, _____
   (gerund phrase)

   _____ , costs nothing but gives me hours of enjoyment.

6. There was only one **way** to convince him — _____
   *(infinitive phrase without **to**)*

   _____ .

7. She left a **message** on his voicemail, _____
   (noun clause)

   _____ .

8. _____

   _____ , **David** would always win the sprinting events at the track meets.

9. Diane bought two new **books** at the sale, _____
   (pronoun)
   _____ and _____ .
   (pronoun)

10. We enjoyed the New Hampshire **scenery**: _____

    _____ and _____ .

EXERCISE F: reading for appositives

Accuracy _____

Directions: Now, read in a good book and find three sentences containing appositives. Write out the sentences below. Also tell the title of the book and its author.

_____

_____

_____

_____

_____

_____

_____

_____

_____

_____

_____

_____

_____

_____

Title and Author: _____

FUNCTION OF THE NOUN IN THE SENTENCE

Subject
common noun   *My sister* will travel to South America next month.
proper noun   *The Boston Red Sox* won the World Series in 2013.
infinitive phrase   *To set goals* is the first step toward success.
gerund phrase   *Playing the bagpipes well* takes years of practice.
noun clause   *Which band we should hire* was the first committee decision.

Direct object
common noun   We built *our tree house* in the tallest oak.
proper noun   Timmy found *Lassie* after a long search.
infinitive phrase   I tried *to remember the combination to my locker*.
gerund phrase   She enjoyed *looking at the old photographs in the family album*.
noun clause   The teacher suggested *that we review our notes*.

Indirect object
common noun   He bought *his little brother* an ice cream cone.
proper noun   We gave *the old Cadillac* a thorough waxing.
gerund phrase   I gave *running for class president* a lot of thought.

Object of the preposition
common noun   The smoke billowed from *the windows*.
proper noun   I bought a ticket to *Seattle*.
infinitive phrase   There was nothing left to do except *surrender our guns*.
gerund phrase   They claim they won by *tracking the winning numbers for two years*.
noun clause   That had nothing to do with *why she received the promotion*.

Subject complement
common noun   My roommate in college became *an acrobat in the circus*.
proper noun   Their dream car was *a 1937 Packard*.
infinitive phrase   My dream is *to play hockey in the Stanley Cup finals and win*.
gerund phrase   My dream is *playing hockey in the Stanley Cup finals and winning*.
noun clause   The interviewer's first question was *why I wanted to work for her company*.

Appositive
common noun   My favorite dish, *fried clams*, was not on the menu.
proper noun   Your sister *Linda* has a crush on me.
infinitive phrase   His promise *to get home before eleven* became impossible to keep.
gerund phrase   My hobby, *fly tying*, keeps me dreaming of the "big one."
noun clause   Who asked the question "*How do I love thee?*"

There are three other ways that a noun can function in a sentence. It may be an **object complement**, a **noun of direct address**, or a **modifier**. The difference between these functions and the functions on the previous page, however, is that these will almost always be common or proper nouns, not phrases or clauses. For a full understanding of nouns, and for application to foreign languages, you should be familiar with these functions.

1. **Object complement:** Sometimes the meaning of a direct object is incomplete without an additional noun after it. Verbs such as *appoint, believe, build, call, choose, consider, designate, elect, make, name, paint,* and *think* often require an object complement.

   I considered him *my best friend*.
   The committee named Cynthia *a representative to the delegation*.

   While we are discussing object complements, we should mention that adjectives may also be object complements.

   I decided to paint the shutters *green*.
   The clatter of the roller coaster made me *nervous*.

2. **Noun of direct address:** When you speak to someone directly, usually in conversation, you are using what is called a noun of direct address. On rare, very informal occasions, it might be a pronoun. Nouns of direct address should be set off from the rest of the sentence by commas.

   "*Mr. Chairman*, I move that the motion be accepted."
   "Listen, *you*, keep your hands off my calculator!"
   "I love you, *Mom*."

3. **Noun as modifier:** It is not unusual for a noun to become a modifier of another noun in a sentence, taking on the function of an adjective. Often the two nouns go so naturally together that we consider them a single noun unit.

   I canceled my *magazine* subscription.
   How do you like my new *leather* jacket?
   He is studying to become a *computer* programmer.

NOUNS

Name: _____

EXERCISE G: nouns in the sentence

Accuracy _____

Directions: In the sentences below, put parentheses around the complete noun unit that is serving the function indicated by the heading. Then in the space tell what that noun unit is, using the appropriate letter:

A=common noun   B=proper noun   C=infinitive phrase   D=gerund phrase   E=noun clause

SUBJECT

1. _____ To tell a real dollar bill from a counterfeit one takes a keen eye.

2. _____ Every apple in the barrel had to be thrown away.

3. _____ Larry Bird might have been the best Boston Celtics player ever.

4. _____ Counting your chickens before they are hatched can lead to disappointment.

5. _____ Wherever you want to plant the tree will be fine with me.

DIRECT OBJECT

6. _____ No one wants to pay too much for a car.

7. _____ I just bought a new watch from a nice old man on the street corner.

8. _____ I have always enjoyed writing with a fountain pen.

9. _____ All of us wondered why the child was standing alone in the corner of the room.

10. _____ She announced at the party that she would be moving to Atlanta.

INDIRECT OBJECT

11. _____ I showed my nephew how to balance a broomstick on his chin.

12. _____ She gave what she should do next a lot of thought.

13. _____ The coach bought every player on the team an ice cream cone.

14. _____ My grandfather wrote President Kennedy a recommendation to Harvard.

15. _____ You should have given learning the multiplication tables a little more attention.

OBJECT OF THE PREPOSITION

16. _____ The radio announcer said she had two tickets for whoever was caller number five.

17. _____ From public speaking we gain confidence and poise.

18. _____ In spite of having an all-American center forward, we still lost.

19. _____ They did everything but score.

20. _____ There was great speculation about how the magician did such amazing tricks.

SUBJECT COMPLEMENT

21. _____ My first question was what we should do about the missing hamster.

22. _____ Our focus became simply to stay alive in the desert.

23. _____ That noise could have been a bear.

24. _____ With my pants ripped and my shoes muddy, I looked a mess.

25. _____ Our first clue should have been the fact that she had grease on her jacket.

APPOSITIVE

26. _____ Herman Melville's famous novel *Moby Dick* was little known while he was alive.

27. _____ Mom's question, where I had been until midnight, seemed reasonable.

28. _____ We fixated on one idea, to get to camp by sundown.

29. _____ The tiny porcelain figurine, a seal balancing a ball, fell and broke.

30. _____ There was a simple explanation, that he just never heard the bell.

NOUNS

Name: _____

EXERCISE H: writing noun units   Accuracy _____ Creativity _____

Directions: Use the following complete noun units in sentences that you create, as directed. Make sure that you are using them as nouns, not as verbs or adjectives. You will be graded on both accuracy and creativity.

Incorrect:	We were *watching the beautiful sunset.*	(main verb)
Incorrect:	*Watching the beautiful sunset*, we fell asleep.	(participial phrase modifying *we*)
Correct:	*Watching the beautiful sunset* made us fall asleep.	(subject of *made*)

WATCHING THE BEAUTIFUL SUNSET

1. (subject) _____

   _____

2. (direct object) _____

   _____

3. (object of preposition) _____

   _____

MINDING MY OWN BUSINESS

4. (direct object) _____

   _____

5. (object of preposition) _____

   _____

6. (appositive) _____

   _____

TO FIND AN AFFORDABLE HOTEL

7. (subject) _____

   _____

8. (direct object) _____

   _____

9. (subject complement) _____

   _____

THAT EVERYONE WAS ALREADY ON THE FIELD

10. (subject) _____

_____

11. (direct object) _____

_____

HOW WE COULD GET IT DONE MORE QUICKLY

12. (direct object) _____

_____

13. (appositive) _____

_____

THE FACT THAT IT WAS ACCIDENTAL

14. (subject) _____

_____

15. (object of preposition) _____

_____

WHERE TO BUILD THE SNOW FORT

16. (subject) _____

_____

17. (direct object) _____

_____

18. (appositive) _____

_____

WHERE THE FARMER PLANTED THE SEEDS

19. (subject) _____

_____

20. (object of preposition) _____

_____

NOUNS

Name: _____

EXERCISE I: all kinds of nouns Accuracy _____ Creativity _____

Directions: Fill in the blanks below with nouns of the given construction and function in the sentence. You may include additional modifiers that are useful and appropriate in order to make a complete noun unit. Notice that you will be graded on both accuracy and creativity.

1. _____ carved his initials on a branch of the apple tree.
   (common noun, subject)

2. _____ is my favorite movie of all time.
   (proper noun, subject)

3. When you are hungry, _____
   (gerund phrase, subject)
   _____ can seem to take forever.

4. _____
   (noun clause, subject)
   _____ was a mystery to me.

5. After much deliberation, I finally bought _____ .
   (proper noun, direct object)

6. At the last minute we decided _____ .
   (infinitive phrase, direct object)

7. Last summer I learned _____ .
   (infinitive phrase, direct object)

8. None of them knew _____ .
   (noun clause, direct object)

9. The vet gave _____ a rabies shot.
   (common noun, indirect object)

10. She gave _____
    (gerund phrase, indirect object)
    _____ her best effort.

11. You had better give _____
    (noun clause, indirect object)
    _____ a little more thought.

12. After the accident I remembered nothing except _____
      (gerund phrase, object of the preposition)

_____ .

13. We discovered the thief by _____
      (noun clause, object of the preposition)

_____ .

14. My role model has always been _____ .
      (common or proper noun, subject complement)

15. Their feeble excuse was _____ .
      (noun clause, subject complement)

16. After that his goal in life became _____
      (infinitive phrase, subject complement)

_____ .

17. She thought up the perfect name for her science project: _____
      (proper noun, appositive)

_____ .

18. My favorite winter activity, _____
      (gerund phrase, appositive)

_____ , costs very little.

19. The topic for her history paper, " _____
      (noun clause, appositive)

_____ ," proved to be a difficult one.

20. Her explanation, _____
      (noun clause, appositive)

_____ , seemed believable.

3. ADJECTIVES

Adjectives provide us with information about nouns and pronouns. Like nouns, adjectives may be single words or larger, more elaborate groups of words. The simplest adjectives are called **articles**, and there are three of them: *a*, *an*, and *the*.

While these articles give little information, they do imply that we have not spoken of the noun before ("Once upon a time there was *a* boy...") or that we have mentioned the noun previously ("One morning *the* boy...").

More specific adjectives begin to give useful information about a noun or pronoun. The adjective might describe, show ownership, give a comparison, tell the place in a sequence, indicate number, or otherwise distinguish this noun or pronoun from others.

big	*empty*	*yellow*	*several*	*darker*	*my*
five	*tenth*	*expensive*	*fastest*	*these*	*no*

THE INFINITIVE PHRASE

In order to create some of our more elaborate adjectives, we again look to the verb forms we have already studied. In the previous chapter we learned how the infinitive could be used as a noun. Let us now look at its use as an adjective.

The infinitive may appear alone or as part of an infinitive phrase. As it did when it was a noun, it may have its own modifiers, complements, or objects. Also, the infinitive may sometimes appear without the word *to*.

We had every reason *to go*.
My chance *to win* was one in a million.
We watched the sailboat *[to] sink*.

His efforts *to quiet his baby brother* were amusing but fruitless.
Everything *to do before Friday* was posted on the refrigerator.
We collected newspaper *to be recycled by the Ecology Club*.

THE PREPOSITIONAL PHRASE

The next grammatical unit acting as an adjective is the prepositional phrase. See Chapter 5 for a list of common prepositions. In that chapter we will look more closely at the many specific roles of the prepositional phrase, but for now simply understand that it may be used as an adjective. Another name for the prepositional phrase used as an adjective is the **adjective phrase**.

Not everyone *from Holland* wears wooden shoes.
The author *of the best-selling novel* was giving autographs.
The twins *in matching outfits* simply couldn't be told apart.

THE PRESENT PARTICIPIAL PHRASE

The next set of adjectives comes from the present participle form of the verb. While these might look very much like the gerunds you have learned about, you must keep in mind that gerunds were nouns, not adjectives. The present participial phrase gives us more information about nouns and pronouns, as all adjectives do, and it also is able to go in several places in the sentence, thus adding new stylistic possibilities to your writing.

The present participle form of a verb, you recall, ends in *-ing*: *being, going, hearing, having*. It is used in combination with forms of the verb *to be* to make the progressive tenses (page 8).

> The children are *squealing.*
> The snow had been *falling.*
> My dog was *howling.*

With a simple rearrangement of the words, we can begin to talk about *the squealing children, the falling snow,* and *my howling dog.* The present participle verb form has become an adjective.

> The *squealing* children seem to enjoy the new gym equipment.
> We watched the *falling* snow as it cast a magical mood over Main Street.
> Mr. Hanson was kept awake all night by my *howling* dog.

As a verb, the present participle is often followed by a prepositional phrase, a direct object, even a noun clause. Let's begin with a simple example.

> The duchess was *walking in the garden.*

If we wished to use the italicized words as a modifier, we could not place it in the usual adjective "slot" between the article and the noun it modifies. We would not write *The walking in the garden duchess....* Instead, we might begin a sentence with the modifier, or place it right after the noun it modifies.

> *Walking in the garden,* the duchess noticed that the roses were beginning to bloom.
> The duchess, *walking in the garden,* noticed that the roses were beginning to bloom.

Each of these modifiers is now called a **present participial phrase**. Here are two more examples of how a present participle verb form becomes a present participial phrase.

> The scuba diver was *picking up shells from the ocean floor.*
> The scuba diver, *picking up shells from the ocean floor,* discovered a Spanish coin.

> He was *thinking that he would never see her again.*
> He looked longingly into her eyes, *thinking that he would never see her again.*

Note: The present participle *having* may combine with a past participle verb form, to produce what is called the **present perfect participle**.

> *Having finished our chores,* we headed off to the swimming pool.

Grammar alert: Make sure that the participial phrase actually has a noun or pronoun to modify, and that it is clear what it is modifying. A **dangling modifier** has nothing to modify, and a **misplaced modifier** is too far away from what it modifies and seems to modify something else.

| **Dangling:** | Skiing down the mountain, the view was wonderful. |
| **Correct:** | Skiing down the mountain, we enjoyed the wonderful view. |

Misplaced:	I saw the cutest family of ducks walking to school yesterday.
Correct:	Walking to school yesterday, I saw the cutest family of ducks.
Correct:	As I was walking to school yesterday, I saw the cutest family of ducks.

THE PAST PARTICIPIAL PHRASE

Like the present participle, the past participle may be used as an adjective. While the present participle tells what a noun or pronoun is or was *doing*, the past participle tells what *was done* to a noun or pronoun. (Notice that *doing* and *done* are the present participle and past participle forms of *do*, respectively.)

The past participle form of a verb has several possible endings: *-ed, -en, -t, -n, -d,* and others. It is used in combination with forms of the verb *to have* to make the perfect tenses (page 8).

The dog has *ripped* my science report.
They had *stolen* the painting.
He has *made* the bookcase by hand.

Again, we may easily take this information and refer to *my ripped science report, the stolen painting,* and *the handmade bookcase.* The past participle verb form has become an adjective.

I easily mended my *ripped* science report with Scotch tape.
The police found the *stolen* painting in a dumpster nearby.
His *handmade* bookcase sold quickly at the craft fair.

As you learned in Chapter 1, "Verbs," the past participle is also the form used to create the passive voice (page 13). Here is a sentence in the passive voice.

The peaches were *nearly frozen by the sudden drop in temperature*.

The italicized words may be removed to become an adjective called a **past participial phrase**.

Nearly frozen by the sudden drop in temperature, the peaches brought
only a fraction of their value at the market.

Here are two more examples of how a past participle verb form becomes a past participial phrase.

The house was *destroyed in the hurricane*.
Destroyed in the hurricane, the house lay in ruins by the sea.

His uncle was *taken hostage by the hijackers*.
Taken hostage by the hijackers, my uncle was barely able to escape.

Like the present participial phrase, the past participial phrase may often be written at more than one place in the sentence. Here are two variations on the above example.

My uncle, *taken hostage by the hijackers*, endured twenty-four hours of pure fear.
My uncle had quite a vacation, first *taken hostage by the hijackers*, then *lost in the Sahara Desert*, and finally *bitten by a snake in the Amazon*.

A sentence may contain two consecutive participial phrases, one a past and one a present.

Drenched by the rain and trailing by two runs, our team was delighted when the umpire called off the game after the third inning.

Grammar alert: As was the case with the present participial phrase, make sure that the past participial phrase actually has a noun or pronoun to modify, and that it is clear what it is modifying.

Dangling:	Exhausted by the hike up the mountain, the lodge was a welcome sight.
Correct:	Exhausted by the hike up the mountain, we welcomed the sight of the lodge.

Misplaced:	Destroyed by the bombs, we wept for the city.
Correct:	We wept for the city destroyed by the bombs.

THE INFINITIVE PHRASE: SAMPLES

She never let a chance escape her *to point out the shortcomings of other tribal groups to the greater glory of our own*, a habit that amused Jem rather than annoyed him.

—Harper Lee, *To Kill a Mockingbird*

In the wild state [otters] will play alone for hours with any convenient floating object in the water, pulling it down to let it bob up again, or throwing it with a jerk of the head so that it lands with a splash and becomes a quarry *to be pursued*.

—Gavin Maxwell, *Ring of Bright Water*

Since there was nowhere *to sleep in the port*, Joseph hired some reporters from among the young men loafing around the trading post and we left right away for Olinka, some four days march through the bush.

—Alice Walker, *The Color Purple*

The grass was so cool and soft to our feet, the air so sweet, and the freedom *to do as we liked was so pleasant* — *to gallup, to lie down, and roll over on our backs, and to nibble the sweet grass*.

—Anna Sewall, *Black Beauty*

When it is 75 below zero, a man must not fail in his first attempt *to build a fire*.

—Jack London, "To Build a Fire"

THE PRESENT PARTICIPIAL PHRASE: SAMPLES

Landing on his knees, hugging the ball, he urged himself to ignore the pain.
— Robert Cormier, *The Chocolate War*

The first man, *picking up the end and threading it through the loop of his leg iron*, stood up then, and, *shuffling a little*, brought the chain tip to the next prisoner, who did the same.
— Toni Morrison, *Beloved*

And as usual, Tessa gathered her books, *lingering behind her classmates, hoping for a conversation she could join*.
— Steven Levenkron, *Kessa*

Douglas shut his eyes and saw the idiot suns *dancing on the reverse side of the pinkly translucent lids*.
— Ray Bradbury, *Dandelion Wine*

Lessa curled into a tight knot of bones, *hugging herself to ease the strain across her tense shoulders*.
— Anne McCaffrey, *Dragonflight*

Liliana and Mavis were right in front of Betsey, *talking the talk she couldn't make sense of*.
— Ntozake Shange, *Betsey Brown*

THE PAST PARTICIPIAL PHRASE: SAMPLES

Relieved that she had nailed him down at last, she feels free to go on with more serious, motherly questions.

— Judith Guest, *Ordinary People*

Frozen with fear, but fascinated, the kid peered over the tops of the boxes and drums as the sedan screeched in, coming to a sideways stop.

— Max Allen Collins, *Dick Tracy*

It stood back from the road, *half hidden among the trees,* through which glimpses could be caught of the wide, cool veranda that ran around its four sides.

— Jack London, *The Call of the Wild*

Having been bitten over a dozen times, Hammond gave up.

— Michael Crichton, *Jurassic Park*

Driven by a stream of salty oaths, and *threatened by the scourging lash of Latinus Mercer,* the slaves gave a good account of themselves and stood firm.

— Clive Cussler, *Treasure*

ADJECTIVES

EXERCISE A: infinitive phrases

Name: _____

Accuracy _____ Creativity _____

Directions: In the spaces below, write infinitive phrases of your own creation. The phrase should modify the noun or pronoun in **bold** print. Notice that you will be graded on both accuracy and creativity.

1. Henry made every **effort** _____

    _____ .

2. The best **way** _____

    _____ had yet to be found.

3. The **candidate** _____

    _____ must have a wide variety of diplomatic skills.

4. Any **attempt** _____

    _____ is sure to be met with enthusiasm.

5. The **fabric** _____

    _____ must cost under eight dollars a yard.

6. We thawed out the **pork chops** _____ .

7. Serving on this committee requires a **willingness** _____ and

    _____ .

8. We both saw the **prisoner** _____
       (infinitive phrase, without the **to***)*

    and _____ .
       (infinitive phrase, without the **to***)*

9. She had high **hopes** _____

    _____ .

10. Now there is **nothing** _____

    _____ .

EXERCISE B: reading for infinitives

Accuracy _____

Directions: Read in a good book and find two sentences containing infinitive phrases being used as adjectives (not as adverbs). Write the sentences below. Be able to tell what noun or pronoun the infinitive phrase is modifying. Also tell the book's title and author.

_____

_____

_____

_____

_____

_____

_____

_____

_____

_____

_____

_____

Title and Author: _____

ADJECTIVES

Name: _____

EXERCISE C: present participial phrases   Accuracy _____ Creativity _____

Directions: Fill in the blanks with present participial phrases of your own creation. The phrase should modify the noun or pronoun in **bold** print.

1. Any **resident** _____
   _____ should report it to the police.

2. Please tell the **girl** _____
   _____ that her sister is waiting for her outside.

3. The silver trophy will go to the **team** _____ _____ .

4. Most **people**, not _____
   _____ , will hang up within the first five seconds.

5. _____
   _____ , the national **flag** inspired the Olympic athletes.

6. _____
   _____ , I was finally allowed to get behind the wheel of the family car.

7. _____
   _____ , the **water** finally wore a hole through the rock.

8. **They** just stood there, _____
   _____ .

9. **We** enjoyed ourselves all day long, _____ and
   _____ until it was time to go home.

10. The **hang glider** stayed aloft for nearly three hours, _____
    _____ , _____
    _____ , and finally _____ .

EXERCISE D: reading for present participial phrases   **Accuracy** _____

Directions: Read in a good book and find at least two sentences that demonstrate the use of the present participial phrase as an adjective (not as the main verb). Be able to tell what noun or pronoun the phrase is modifying. Write the sentences below. Also tell the book's title and author.

_____

_____

_____

_____

_____

_____

_____

_____

_____

_____

_____

_____

_____

Title and Author: _____

ADJECTIVES

EXERCISE E: past participial phrases

Name: _____

Accuracy _____ Creativity _____

Directions: Fill in the blanks with past participial phrases of your own creation. The phrase should modify the noun or pronoun in **bold** print.

1. The **table** _____

   _____ brought almost $12,000 at the auction.

2. _____

   _____ , the **race car driver** settled into the driver's seat.

3. I looked at the tree's last remaining **leaf**, _____

   _____ .

4. The vendor's **pushcart**, _____

   _____ , lay splintered and useless.

5. _____ , the **plumber** frantically fumbled with the gushing faucet.

6. The **coach**, _____ but not yet

   _____ , gave a rousing halftime speech to the players.

7. Having _____

   _____ , **we** set out on our long-awaited summer vacation.

8. _____ and losing air speed rapidly,

   the **pilot** radioed a mayday message.

9. Most **people** _____

   _____ will probably just hang up.

10. The **boxer** lay on the canvas, _____

   and _____ .

EXERCISE F: reading for past participial phrases

Accuracy _____

Directions: Read in a good book and find at least two sentences that demonstrate the use of the past participial phrase as an adjective. Be able to tell what noun or pronoun the phrase is modifying. Write the sentences below. Also tell the book's title and author.

_____

_____

_____

_____

_____

_____

_____

_____

_____

_____

_____

_____

_____

Title and Author: _____

THE ADJECTIVE CLAUSE

The final category of adjectives is the **adjective clause**, a group of words containing a verb and a subject to go with it, modifying a noun or pronoun.

Using an adjective clause is a useful way to join two sentences that have a noun or pronoun in common. One of the sentences we will call the *receiver sentence*. It will "receive" the other sentence but will not itself change. The other sentence will be the *donor sentence*. It will "donate" its information to the receiver sentence, but first it has to undergo some changes. Just strike out the repeated words and substitute the relative pronoun or adverb.

An adjective clause usually begins with one of the following:

a **relative pronoun**   *who, whose, whom, which, that*
or a **relative adverb**   *where, when, why*

Receiver sentence:	Sara Phillips hands out the best candy at Halloween.
Donor sentence:	~~Sara Phillips~~ lives just next door.
Relative pronoun:	**who**
Final sentence:	Sara Phillips, *who lives just next door*, gives the best candy at Halloween.
Receiver sentence:	The contestant will win a CD.
Donor sentence:	~~The contestant's~~ name will be drawn from the barrel.
Relative pronoun:	**whose**
Final sentence:	The contestant *whose name will be drawn from the barrel* will win a CD.
Receiver sentence:	The man loves children.
Donor sentence:	I am engaged to ~~the man~~.
Relative pronoun:	**whom**
Final sentence:	The man *to whom I am engaged* loves children.
Receiver sentence:	Every flower died.
Donor sentence:	She planted ~~every flower~~.
Relative pronoun:	**which/that**
Final sentence:	Every flower *which/that she planted* died.
Receiver sentence:	I'll never forget the restaurant.
Donor sentence:	We first ate Thai food ~~at the restaurant~~.
Relative adverb:	**where**
Final sentence:	I'll never forget the restaurant *where we first ate Thai food*.
Receiver sentence:	Nobody was at the cabin on the day.
Donor sentence:	We arrived ~~on the day~~.
Relative adverb:	**when**
Final sentence:	Nobody was at the cabin on the day *when we arrived*.

Sometimes a relative pronoun may stand for a full sentence.

I bought the first pair of shoes I tried on, *which proved to be a mistake.*

What was the mistake? *(The fact that) I bought the first pair of shoes I tried on.*

ADJECTIVE CLAUSE ISSUES

Grammar alert: Deciding whether to use *who* or *whom* is easy when you determine what the word it is replacing did in the donor sentence. If it was the subject or predicate nominative, then use *who*. If it was the direct or indirect object, or object of the preposition, then use *whom*.

Punctuation alert: Like an appositive, sometimes an adjective clause is set off from the rest of the sentence by commas, and sometimes it is not. If the noun or pronoun is clear to the reader without the adjective clause, then it may be set off. But if the adjective clause provides important information, separating one from many, then it must not be set off by commas.

> My aunt, *who lives in Chicago,* is coming to visit.   (I have only the one aunt.)
> My aunt *who lives in Chicago* is coming to visit.   (I have more than one aunt.)

Omitted relative pronoun: Sometimes the relative pronoun or relative adverb may be omitted. Look at the examples given on the previous page and see where that can be done.

Summary: Here is an illustration of how one noun, *canoe*, may be modified by an array of adjectives.

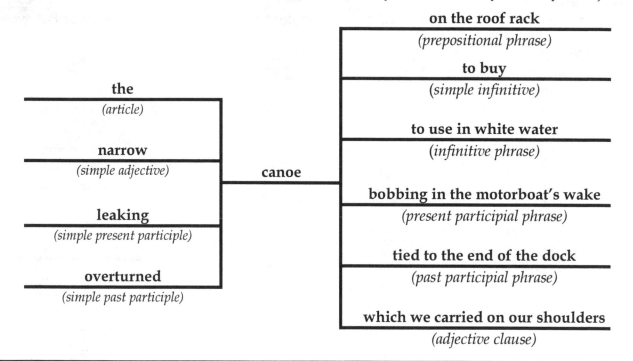

	on the roof rack
	(prepositional phrase)
the	to buy
(article)	*(simple infinitive)*
narrow	to use in white water
(simple adjective)	*(infinitive phrase)*
canoe	bobbing in the motorboat's wake
leaking	*(present participial phrase)*
(simple present participle)	tied to the end of the dock
overturned	*(past participial phrase)*
(simple past participle)	which we carried on our shoulders
	(adjective clause)

THE ADJECTIVE CLAUSE: SAMPLES

Night, *whose name just frightened me by the sound of it,* was giving the crew a tongue lashing.
— Clive Cussler, *Treasure*

He took up his overcoat from the chair *where he had thrown it.*
— Agatha Christie, *The Mystery of the Blue Train*

The two kids *that I had seen before* left early, *which seemed very strange to me.*   — James Herbert, *Fog*

ADJECTIVES

Name: _____

EXERCISE G: adjective clauses

Accuracy _____ Creativity _____

Directions: In the spaces below, write adjective clauses of your own creation. Put commas where they are appropriate. The clauses should modify the words in **bold** print. Notice that all of number 5 is in bold print.

1. **Edgar Allan Poe** _____

_____

attended West Point for a short time.

2. Any **student** _____

_____ will have to fill out these forms.

3. Everyone look at that **boy** in the front row _____

_____ .

4. You may return any **shirt** _____

_____ .

5. **I couldn't get my hands all the way around the rope,** _____

_____ .

6. Isn't this the **pond** _____

_____ ?

7. I have circled on my calendar the **day** _____

_____ .

8. **The Leaning Tower of Pizza** _____

_____ fell down last night.

9. I finally met **Liam O'Grady** _____

_____ .

10. She is a **woman** _____

but _____ .

EXERCISE H: reading for adjective clauses   **Accuracy** _____

Directions: Now, read in a good book and find three sentences that contain adjective clauses. Be able to tell what noun or pronoun the clause is modifying. Write the sentences below. Also tell the book's title and author.

_____

_____

_____

_____

_____

_____

_____

_____

_____

_____

_____

_____

Title and Author: _____

ADJECTIVES

Name: _____

EXERCISE I: adjective review

Accuracy _____ Creativity _____

Directions: Fill in the blanks below with adjectives modifying the noun or pronoun in **bold** print. Where would you put it? Would you use commas? You do not need to rewrite the original sentence.

1. The **chicken** did not look very appetizing.

   _____ past part. phrase

   _____ adjective clause

2. **Mr. Davis** chased us all the way to the golf course.

   _____ and _____ 2 simple adject.

   _____ pres. part. phrase

   _____ adjective clause

3. The Highway Department planted **trees** along our street.

   _____ and _____ 2 simple adject.

   _____ past part. phrase

   _____ adjective clause

4. We'll give a complimentary pair of tickets to **anyone.**

   _____ pres. part. phrase

   _____ adjective clause

5. My brand new **tennis racquet** broke the first time I used it.

   _____ past part. phrase

   _____ adjective clause

6. The best **fishing lure** is the jitterbug.

   _____ prep. phrase

   _____ infinitive phrase

7. Some inexperienced **athletes** will quit rather than face the embarrassment of defeat.

   _____ and   two pres. part.

   _____ phrases

   _____ past part. phrase

   _____ infinitive phrase

8. The **coffee table** was a welcome addition to our living room.

   _____ past part. phrase

   _____ adjective clause

ADJECTIVES

Name: _____

EXERCISE J: adjectives of all kinds   **Accuracy** _____ **Creativity** _____

Directions: Fill in the blanks below with adjectives as indicated and modifying the noun or pronoun in **bold** print. Notice that you will be graded on both accuracy and creativity.

1. _____ _____**computer** needs to be repaired.
   (article)   *(simple past participle)*

2. The **supermarket** _____ stays open all night.
   (prepositional phrase)

3. The _____ **photograph** _____
   (simple past participle)   *(prepositional phrase)*

   _____ was all the police needed to arrest him.

4. _____ , **we** noticed that the barn was on fire.
   (present participial phrase)

5. The **referee**, _____ , blew the whistle
   (past participial phrase)
   on _____ _____ **bump**.
      (simple adjective)   *(simple adjective)*

6. The _____ **student** _____
   (simple adjective)   *(adjective clause)*

   _____ will have to stay after school.

7. I promptly lost the _____ **jacket** _____
   (simple past participle)   *(adjective clause)*

   _____ .

8. The _____ **costume** _____
   (simple adjective)   *(infinitive phrase)*

   is not always the one _____ .
                          (adjective clause)

9. The _____ **plumber** finally fixed the **faucet** _____
   (simple past participle)   *(adjective clause)*

   _____ .

10. **You** seem _____ today.
    (infinitive phrase)

4. ADVERBS

Adverbs provide information about verbs, adjectives, or other adverbs. Like nouns and adjectives, adverbs may be single words or larger, more elaborate groups of words.

As modifiers of verbs, adverbs answer several kinds of questions.

We ride the bus	**(when?)**	*every morning.*
	(where?)	*into the city.*
	(how?)	*reluctantly.*
	(why?)	*because it saves us money.*
	(under what conditions?)	*in spite of the crowds.*

As modifiers of adjectives or adverbs, adverbs usually answer the questions **how? when?** or **how much?**

The math problems were *rather* easy.	**(how** easy?)
This jacket was *not* expensive.	**(how** expensive?)
Seldom late, Jack was a good worker.	**(when** late?)
His *very* dark blue eyes intrigued me.	**(how** dark?)
The roof was *almost* completely gone.	**(how much** completely?)

The simplest adverbs are single words. Many of them are made by adding *-ly* to an adjective. Others have little connection with adjectives.

tight/tightly	*high/highly*	*slow/slowly*
typical/typically	*nervous/nervously*	*bad/badly*
rather	*very*	*up*
seldom	*often*	*out*

THE INFINITIVE PHRASE

For the third time, we call upon the infinitive form of the verb to be a different part of speech. First it served as a noun, then as an adjective, and now we will use it as an adverb, again either by itself or as an infinitive phrase, with its own modifiers and complements. It will usually be answering the question **why?** or **how?** In each of these examples, determine what the infinitive is modifying.

| We went to Colorado *to ski.* |
| The new sales clerk was eager *to please.* |
| You are too young *to go.* |

| I was delighted *to get your letter.* |
| Their scores were too close *to make any difference.* |
| I printed *to make sure he would be able to read it.* |

THE PREPOSITIONAL PHRASE

We have already seen the prepositional phrase used as an adjective, called an adjective phrase. The prepositional phrase may also be used as an adverb, and logically will be called an **adverb phrase.** See Chapter 5 for a list of common prepositions. In that chapter we will look more closely at the many roles of the prepositional phrase, but here we will simply examine how it acts as an adverb, modifying verbs, adjectives, or other adverbs.

The alligator slithered *into the river.*	(slithered **where?)**
The dishes had all been sold *before your arrival.*	(sold **when?)**
The wreath looks great *on the front door.*	(great **where?)**
I waded along the shore in my jeans, wet *from the knees down.*	(wet **where?)**
The engine ran quieter *with a drop of well-placed oil.*	(quieter **why?)**
She opened the present carefully, *like an archeologist in King Tut's tomb.*	**(how** carefully?)

As may be seen from the last example above, it is sometimes difficult to tell exactly which word the prepositional phrase is modifying.

Is she like an archeologist?

or

Did she open the present carefully, the way an archeologist in King
Tut's tomb would do things carefully?

What we have here is a **sentence modifier,** a phrase that helps the reader visualize both the subject of the sentence and the way in which the verb is being performed. Such comparisons, often beginning with *like* or *as*, give a much clearer picture of the entire idea being expressed in the main clause.

THE ADVERB CLAUSE

The final category of adverbs is the adverb clause. Like the other clauses, it contains a verb and a subject to go with it. It will usually answer questions about the verb in the main clause.

When:	*After we finished washing the outside of the car*, we vacuumed the interior.
Why:	*Cars stood at a standstill at the intersection*, because the traffic lights were not working.
How:	*As if he were playing a video game*, he weaved through the traffic.
Under what conditions:	*If you help me clean out the garage,* I'll take you out for ice cream.

The adverb clause may also modify an adjective.

They were happy *that we could attend the barbecue.*

And the adverb clause may also modify an adverb.

She ran faster *than she had ever run before.*

Often the adverb clause appears in the form *as.....as,* with either an adjective or an adverb appearing in the middle.

> The sand castle was *as big as we could make it.*
> We left *as soon as the concert was over.*

By studying the examples, you will see that the process of constructing an adverb clause is quite simple. All that is needed is to add a subordinating conjunction (A) at the beginning of the sentence you wish to subordinate (B). Thus an independent clause is transformed into a subordinate, adverb clause (A+B), which you can then attach to another independent clause (C).

A	+	B	C
Although	+	he couldn't see the burglar,	he knew he was in the room.
Before	+	the shutters could be painted,	we had to scrape and sand them.
			We'll have plenty of room at the cabin,
unless	+	our in-laws drop in unexpectedly.	
			She stood with her shoulders sagging,
as though	+	she had lost her best friend.	

Common subordinating conjunctions: *after, although, as, because, before, if, lest, once, since, than, that, though, till, unless, until, when(ever), where(ever), whereas, whether, while, why.*

Sometimes two or more words are used to form a subordinating conjunction: *as if, as soon as, as though, even if, even though, in case, in order that, provided that, so that.*

ADVERB CLAUSE ISSUES

1. In Chapter 1, "Verbs," you learned about the subjunctive mood, which is used to express an imaginary situation. The subjunctive mood often appears in an adverb clause, following the subordinating conjunctions *if, as if,* or *as though.* In such cases, the normal forms *I was, he was, she was,* and *it was* become *I were, he were, she were,* and *it were.*

> *If I were you,* I'd buy the red one.
> She looked around *as though she were lost.*
> He stared at the puzzle *as if it were impossible.*

2. You should also note the rather unusual subordinating conjunction *lest,* which means "for fear that." The verb in the adverb clause that follows *lest* should be in the infinitive form. Use *lest* when you do not want that verb to happen.

> I tied a string around my finger, *lest I be late and miss the bus.*

3. Be alert to the punctuation requirements of an adverb clause. When an adverb clause begins a sentence, the clause should be followed by a comma (as in this sentence). An adverb clause at the end of a sentence is usually not preceded by a comma, unless there is a natural pause before it (as in this sentence).

Summary: Here is an illustration of how one verb, *dribbles,* may be modified by an array of adverbs.

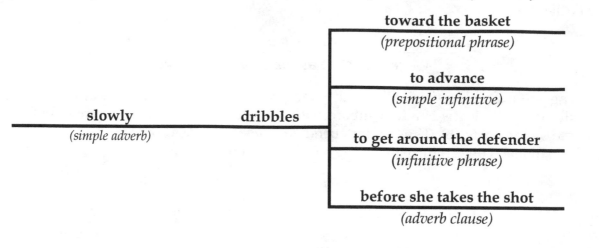

ADVERB CLAUSE: SAMPLES

As I remember, it was one morning a little while *after my father and Miss Kenton had joined the staff,* I had been in my pantry, sitting at the table going through my paperwork, *when I heard a knock at my door.*
— Kazuo Shiguro, *The Remains of the Day*

When I started making big money, I got him to quit his job *so I could take care of him and let him relax.*
— Wayne Gretzky, *An Autobiography*

The variations were more *than the most violent storm was expected to produce.*
— Alan D. Foster, *Midworld*

Will was pleasant to talk to *because he had so little to say and yet was so understanding a listener.*
— Margaret Mitchell, *Gone With the Wind*

Just as his more fortunate fellow New Yorkers had bought their tickets to Palm Beach and the Riviera each winter, so Soapy had made his humble arrangements for his annual hegira to the Island.
— O. Henry, "The Cop and the Anthem"

Dalgliesh was shaken by a pity so unexpected and so acute *that for a moment he dared not speak.*
— P. D. James, *A Taste for Death*

When Fielding entered the doors clapped to, and were guarded by a servant, *while a punkah,* to mark the importance of the moment, *flapped dirty petticoats over their heads.*
— E. M. Forster, *A Passage to India*

Bonny at last understood they were intended for her, took them, looked at him *as if he were playing a trick on her,* then opened the book, read her name in it, and laughed *as if he had asked her a riddle she couldn't answer.*
— Margaret Mahy, *Memory*

ADVERBS

Name: _____

EXERCISE A: adverb clauses   Accuracy _____ Creativity _____

Directions: In the spaces below, write adverb clauses of your own creation. Be thoughtful and varied in your responses.

1. _____

   _____ , he consulted his attorney.

2. _____

   _____ , I will meet you at the waterfront.

3. The carpenter couldn't finish the cabinet _____

   _____ .

4. She stepped along the tightrope, _____

   _____ .

5. His new job was not as _____ as _____
   (simple adjective)

   _____ .

6. He jiggled the fishing line _____

   _____ .

7. We arrived at the party _____ but

   _____ .
   (another adverb clause, not a new sentence)

8. The kitten was so sick _____

   _____ .

9. Our day at the amusement park was more _____ than _____
   (simple adjective)

   _____ .

10. _____ , _____ , and

    _____ — only then will I marry you.

EXERCISE B: reading for adverb clauses

Accuracy _____

Directions: Now, read in a good book and find three sentences that contain adverb clauses. Be able to tell what verb, adjective, or adverb the clause is modifying. Write the sentences below. Also tell the book's title and author.

_____

_____

_____

_____

_____

_____

_____

_____

_____

_____

_____

_____

Title and Author: _____

ADVERBS

Name: _____

EXERCISE C: adverb phrases and clauses   **Accuracy** _____ **Creativity** _____

Directions: Fill in the spaces below with adverbs of the indicated construction, providing the information needed. The words being modified are in **bold** print. Notice that you will be graded on both accuracy and creativity.

1. The chorus **sang** _____ .
    (prepositional phrase, when)

2. We **walked** along _____
    (adverb clause, how)

    _____ .

3. I **called** you _____
    (infinitive phrase, why)

    _____ .

4. She **found** it _____
    (adverb clause, where)

    _____ .

5. I will **take** it _____
    (adverb clause, under what conditions)

    _____ .

6. I **knew** it _____
    (adverb clause, when)

    _____ .

7. Jody was **quick** _____
    (infinitive phrase, how; quick in what way)

    _____ .

8. We stood at the front of the building, **waiting,** _____ .
    (prepositional phrase, why)

9. The mask was scary, **painted** _____
    (infinitive phrase, how)

    _____ .

10. We left the decorations incomplete, to be **finished** _____
    (prepositional phrase, how)

    _____ .

ADVERBS

Name: _____

EXERCISE D: adverbs of all kinds **Accuracy** _____ **Creativity** _____

Directions: Fill in the spaces below with adverbs of the indicated types.

1. We _____understand the impact of a casual remark _____
       (simple adverb)   *(adverb clause)*

   _____ .

2. All the players were determined _____ .
                                          (infinitive phrase)

3. _____ , then we can go
                   (adverb clause, under what conditions)

   _____ .
       (prepositional phrase, where)

4. I can't write _____ _____
            (simple adverb)   *(adverb clause, under what conditions)*

   _____ .

5. The candle maker _____ poured the hot wax _____ .
                (simple adverb)   *(prepositional phrase, where)*

6. She brought her bicycle _____ _____
                  (prepositional phrase, where)   *(adverb clause, why)*

   _____ .

7. _____
                (adverb clause, how)

   _____ , he waved to the crowd.

8. We all grew _____ nervous _____
             (simple adverb)   *(adverb clause, when)*

   _____ .

9. We _____ crowded _____
         (simple adverb)   *(prepositional phrase, where)*

   _____ .
       (infinitive phrase, why)

10. _____ , the rock group
        (prepositional phrase, why)

    _____ had to cancel the show.
     (simple adverb)

5. PREPOSITIONS

A preposition is a word that shows a relationship between a noun or pronoun (called the **object of the preposition**) and another word in the sentence.

Common prepositions: *about, above, across, after, against, along, among, around, as, at, before, behind, below, beneath, beside, besides, between, beyond, but* (except), *by, concerning, down, during, except, for, from, in, into, like, near, of, off, on, out, outside, over, past, round, since, through, till, to, toward, under, underneath, until, up, upon, with, within, without.*

Sometimes two or more words are used to form a preposition: *because of, on account of, by means of, in spite of, apart from, in place of, instead of, according to, out of, as to.*

Earlier in this book you learned that prepositional phrases may be used as adjectives or adverbs. As such, prepositional phrases serve many purposes:

to indicate direction or place	We climbed *toward the summit.* The goldfish swam *in the bowl.*
to establish time relationships	I left *before intermission.* They played *after finishing their homework.*
to provide identification	You should read the report *of the committee.* There was nothing *concerning the budget.*
to make a comparison	Your violin sounds *like a cat stuck in a drainpipe.* He has a beard *like Abraham Lincoln's.*
to provide narrative detail	She entered the water *without a splash.* He pointed to the boats *in a sweeping gesture.*
to provide descriptive detail	He looked silly *without his false teeth.* She stood covered *in green and red paint.*

A **narrative detail** lets the reader see the action of the verb more clearly. A **descriptive detail** lets the reader perceive the noun or pronoun more completely.

The prepositional phrase is usually found immediately after the word it modifies, as in the examples above. But it may also be used to begin or end a sentence, often in combination with other grammatical constructions.

Without a penny between them, my grandparents set out for Alaska.
Like a ballerina playing the dying swan, my sister threw her hand to her forehead and fell onto the couch.
The horse cantered around the corral, *with a magnificent tossing of its head and snorting from its nostrils.*

PREPOSITIONAL PHRASE ISSUES

Compared to what? When making comparisons, make sure they say what you want them to.

Incorrect:	He has a beard *like Abraham Lincoln.*
Correct:	He has a beard *like Abraham Lincoln's.*

The right case? If the object of the preposition is a personal pronoun, make sure it is in the objective case. Chapter 7, "Pronouns," has more practice with pronoun case, but here are some things to know.

They played a great game against *us* boys.
Everyone except *him* received an invitation.
That's a secret between *her* and *me*.
From *whom* did he buy the Model T Ford?

If the object of the preposition is a noun clause, you might again need to determine whether to use *who* or *whom*. Which form to use will be determined by its use in the noun clause, not by the fact that it follows a preposition.

We have no information about *who* was on the train.	**subject of *was***
Our whole senior year depends on *whom* we elect today.	**direct object of *elect***

Preposition or adverb? What might look like a preposition may actually be an adverb, and the noun that follows it is a direct object, not the object of the preposition. Consider these sentences:

He wrote down the license number.
She skied down the mountain.

In the first sentence, *the license number* is the direct object of the verb *wrote down*. In the second sentence, *the mountain* is the object of the preposition *down*.

Usually you can tell the difference by rearranging the word order of the sentence.

He wrote the license number down.

It is now clear that *down* is an adverb, not a preposition. A similar rearrangement of the second sentence would make little sense.

There are several other prepositions that can stand alone as adverbs. Consider these sentences, then try to find others on the preposition list that could also be adverbs.

She put her arms *up*.	It's cold *outside*.	The children ran *around* wildly.

Preposition or conjunction? In the next chapter, you will learn about conjunctions, another part of speech. Many conjunctions also look like prepositions. For now, you should just remember that a preposition is followed by some form of noun or pronoun, creating a prepositional phrase that may then be used as an adjective or an adverb.

Another -*ing* ending? You have learned about the present participle verb form, the present participial phrase, and the gerund phrase. Although they function in very different ways in a sentence, as verb, adjective, and noun, they all end with -*ing*. Now you see *during* and *concerning*. It can get confusing. To remember that *concerning* and *during* are prepositions, try substituting other prepositions in simple prepositional phrases.

concerning the story	*about* the story	*in* the story

during the concert	*before* the concert	*after* the concert

PREPOSITIONS

Name: _____

EXERCISE A: objects of prepositions   Accuracy _____ Creativity _____

Directions: In this exercise, we have provided some prepositions, preceded by words for the prepositional phrases to modify. You need to complete those prepositional phrases by supplying the objects of the prepositions, using the type of noun indicated. You may wish to turn back to Chapter 2 to review nouns. Notice that you will be graded on both accuracy and creativity.

PREPOSITIONAL PHRASES AS ADJECTIVES

1.   A first edition **of** _____
     (common noun)

2.   Every president **since** _____
     (proper noun)

3.   anything **except** _____
     (noun clause)

4.   nobody **apart from** _____
     (proper noun)

5.   great success **without** _____
     (gerund phrase)

6.   no choice **but** _____
     (infinitive phrase)

7.   six members **in addition to** _____
     (common noun)

PREPOSITIONAL PHRASES AS ADVERBS

8.   drove **without** _____
     (gerund phrase)

9.   stood **during** _____
     (proper noun)

10. built **according to** _____
     (noun clause)

11. flew **beyond** _____
     (proper noun)

12. tasted **like** _____
                            (common noun)

13. read **instead of** _____
                            (gerund phrase)

14. missing **since** _____
                            (proper noun)

15. sad **because of** _____
                            (gerund phrase)

16. red **like** _____
                            (common noun)

17. tired **from** _____
                            (gerund phrase)

18. undecided **as to** _____
                            (noun clause)

19. lonesome **without** _____
                            (common noun)

20. hidden **beneath** _____
                            (proper noun)

PREPOSITIONS

Name: _____

EXERCISE B: prepositional phrases

Accuracy _____ Creativity _____

Directions: In this exercise, we have provided only the prepositions. Fill in the blank preceding the preposition with the indicated part of speech. Then, complete the prepositional phrase by writing an object of the preposition in the form indicated, as you did in Exercise A.

EXAMPLES:

____chicken____	*with*	____no feathers____
(noun)		*(common noun)*
____something____	*from*	____Montreal, Canada____
(pronoun)		*(proper noun)*
____will leave____	*instead of*	____hanging around here all day____
(verb)		*(gerund phrase)*
____sold out____	*according to*	____what I read in the paper____
(adjective)		*(noun clause)*

1. _____ *besides* _____
   (noun)   *(gerund phrase)*

2. _____ *but* _____
   (noun)   *(infinitive phrase)*

3. _____ *according to* _____
   (noun)   *(noun clause)*

4. _____ *like* _____
   (pronoun)   *(proper noun)*

5. _____ *out of* _____
   (verb)   *(common noun)*

6. _____ *until* _____
   (verb)   *(proper noun)*

7. _____ *against* _____
   (verb)   *(noun clause)*

8. _____ *by* _____
   (verb)   *(gerund phrase)*

9. _____ *from* _____
   (adjective)   *(gerund phrase)*

10. _____ *because of* _____
    (adjective)   *(noun clause)*

EXERCISE C: prepositional phrases
by purpose

Accuracy _____ Creativity _____

Directions: Fill in the spaces below with prepositional phrases as indicated. Once you have written the prepositional phrase, you may add further information that you feel is appropriate.

1. The senior _____
    (descriptive detail)

    _____ kept giggling throughout the school meeting.

2. No one knew the name _____ .
    (identification)

3. His little sister kept squirting the hose _____ .
    (direction or place)

4. The jet plane smoothly rolled through the 360-degree turn, _____
    (comparison)

    _____ .

5. The yapping dog chased the terrified kitten _____ ,
    (direction)

    _____ , and _____ .
    (direction)   *(direction)*

6. He looked like a pirate, with _____ ,
    (object 1)

    _____ , and _____ .
    (object 2)   *(object 3)*

7. _____
    (time)

    _____ , we loaded the wagon and went home.

8. Her pet hamster, _____
    (time)

    _____ , hopped out of the cage and ran behind the bookcase.

9. Most of the trees _____ will have to be cut down.
    (place)

10. _____
    (comparison)

    _____ , she ran her fingers up and down the piano keys.

PREPOSITIONS

Name: _____

EXERCISE D: reading for prepositional phrases

Accuracy _____

Directions: Read in a good book of fiction and look for ten prepositional phrases being used as **adjectives** (reading for prepositional phrases as adverbs is on the next page: be careful). In the left column, write the word the phrase modifies. In the right column, write the phrase itself. At the bottom, write the name of the book and its author.

Prepositional phrases as adjectives

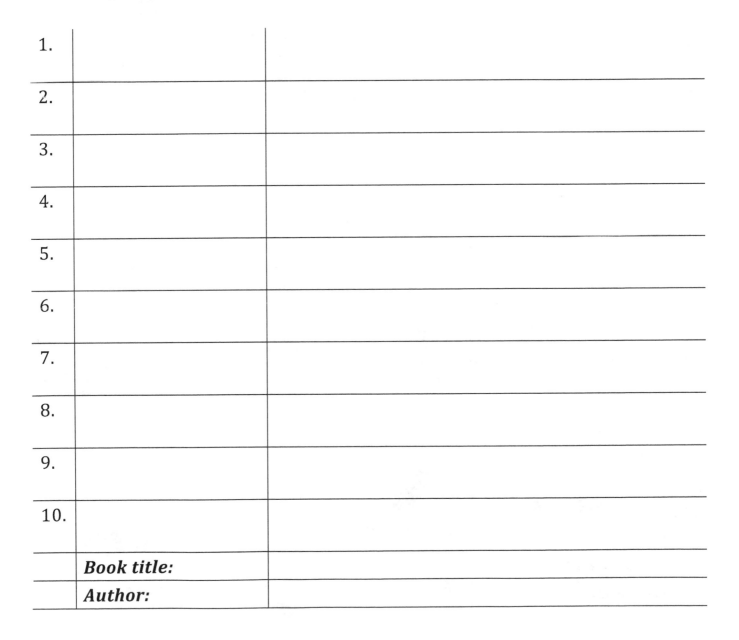

1.		
2.		
3.		
4.		
5.		
6.		
7.		
8.		
9.		
10.		
	Book title:	
	Author:	

PREPOSITIONS

Name: _____

EXERCISE E: reading for prepositional phrases

Accuracy _____

Directions: Read in a good book of fiction and look for ten prepositional phrases being used as **adverbs**. In the left column, write the word the phrase modifies. In the right column, write the phrase itself. At the bottom, write the name of the book and its author. You do not need to use the same book that you used in Exercise D.

Prepositional phrases as adverbs

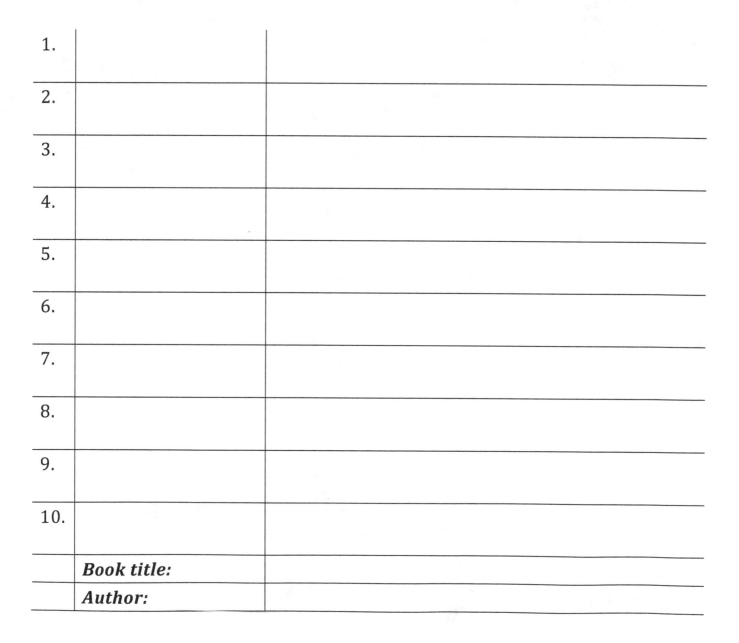

1.		
2.		
3.		
4.		
5.		
6.		
7.		
8.		
9.		
10.		
	Book title:	
	Author:	

6. CONJUNCTIONS AND INTERJECTIONS

CONJUNCTIONS

A **conjunction** is used to join two sentences or two parts of a sentence to each other. There are four different kinds.

1. **Coordinating conjunctions:** These are used to join items that are of equal importance, especially independent clauses. A fun way to learn them is to remember the silly phrase

$$f-a-n-b-o-y-s$$

These letters stand for *for, and, nor, but, or, yet, so.*

Examples:

No one left the fireworks early, **for** we all wanted to see the finale.
Jack **and** Jill went up the hill.
We could not go out to the movies, **nor** could we even watch television.
I found the camera **but** not the tripod.
Come along now **or** you will be left behind.
We promised not to giggle, **yet** he would not get up and dance.
Our money ran out, **so** we had to come home.

2. **Subordinating conjunctions:** You used subordinating conjunctions when you wrote noun clauses and you created a subordinate clause, which could then be attached to another sentence or sentence part.

Examples:

We both know *that* we haven't heard the last of it.	**noun clause**
While you were away, we wallpapered your room.	**adverb clause**

As a reminder, the single-word subordinating conjunctions are *after, although, as, because, before, if, lest, once, since, than, that, though, till, unless, until, when(ever), where(ever), whereas, whether, while,* and *why.*

The subordinating conjunctions that consist of more than one word are *as if, as soon as, as though, even if, even though, in case, in order that, provided that,* and *so that.*

3. **Correlative conjunctions:** These conjunctions come in pairs: *both...and, either...or, neither...nor, not (only)... but (also), whether...or.*

There are two problem areas that arise when you use correlative conjunctions. First, the grammatical construction following both of them must be the same. This is called *parallelism*.

Incorrect:	In Paris we *not only* saw the Eiffel Tower *but also* Notre Dame.
Correct:	In Paris we saw *not only* the Eiffel Tower *but also* Notre Dame.

Second, when you are using *either...or* or *neither...nor* with two subjects of the sentence, and one is singular and the other is plural, your verb should agree with the subject that is closer to the inflected verb (the verb that changes).

Examples:	*Does* either *Bill* or his brothers own a car?
	Do either Bill's *brothers* or he own a car?
	Neither the teacher nor the *students have* an idea where the maps went.
	Neither the students nor the *teacher has* an idea where the maps went.

4. **Conjunctive adverbs:** This unusual term is applied to words that join independent clauses and show a special relationship between the ideas expressed in each sentence. An important punctuation note is that they are preceded by a semicolon, and they will usually be followed by a comma.

   Common conjunctive adverbs: *also, besides, consequently, for example, furthermore, however, in fact, likewise, meanwhile, moreover, nevertheless, otherwise, then, therefore,* and *thus.*

Examples:	We'd love to come to the party; *however,* we won't be able to stay for long.
	You stay here; *meanwhile,* I'll sneak around back.
	She had better mail the letters today; *otherwise,* they'll never get there in time.

Remember that all conjunctions join grammatical units; they themselves are neither modified nor modifiers.

INTERJECTIONS

We have tucked the last part of speech, the **interjection**, into this left-over half page to emphasize its special but limited role in your writing. By definition, an interjection is any word or phrase that is not grammatically related to the sentence but which adds a special mood, attitude, or feeling to the sentence. An interjection might show excitement, casualness, alarm, or intimacy.

Well, I don't know whether I should tell you.
Yikes! That's hot!
Gee, she's a better singer than I thought.

An interjection, as you might gather from the sentences above, is often heard in conversation. It implies an informal tone and therefore should be used with restraint in formal writing. There will be no exercises involving interjections.

CONJUNCTIONS

Name: _____

EXERCISE A: types of conjunctions

Accuracy _____

Directions: Fill in the blanks with appropriate conjunctions. Be careful about which ones you choose, for in many cases only one or a few conjunctions will fit the logic and the grammar of the rest of the sentence. If you are uncertain about the meaning of a particular conjunction, look it up in a dictionary.

COORDINATING CONJUNCTIONS

1. I'd love to visit Ireland _____ Scotland.

2. We don't have much, _____ we are happy.

3. She didn't know the number, _____ could she find it online.

4. I can't leave the house, _____ maybe you can come over.

5. I just put it in the oven, _____ you'll just have to wait.

SUBORDINATING CONJUNCTIONS

6. _____ only twenty people came, we showed the movie anyway.

7. I delivered the check in person _____ it get lost in the mail.

8. _____ you scrape off the old paint, the new paint will not last long.

9. We had to take a detour _____ the road was being repaired.

10. Everyone wished _____ the rain would stop.

CORRELATIVE CONJUNCTIONS

11. _____ my mother _____ my father has ever been to Mexico.

12. _____ spaghetti _____ ziti will be fine with me.

13. I wanted to find out _____ where it was sold _____ how much it cost.

14. _____ you do it _____ I do it myself, it will get done.

15. I had to _____ wash the car _____ vacuum the interior.

CONJUNCTIVE ADVERBS

16. None of us knew our lines on Tuesday; _____ , the show opened successfully

    on Friday.

17. You really don't need a new stereo; _____ , you don't have the money.

18. Please help me with this laundry; _____ , we'll never finish on time.

19. I can start work on your car today; _____ , the parts won't be in until Wednesday.

20. All the public transportation workers are on strike; _____ , we had to walk.

EXERCISE B: reading for conjunctions   Accuracy _____

Directions: Now read in a good book and find one example of each type of conjunction. Write your discoveries below.

   You will probably find a sentence containing a conjunctive adverb more easily in a work of nonfiction than in a work of fiction. Make sure that it is preceded by a semicolon; otherwise, it is only an adverb, not a conjunctive adverb.

(coordinating) _____

_____

_____

(subordinating) _____

_____

_____

(correlative) _____

_____

_____

(conjunctive adverb) _____

_____

_____

Title and Author: _____

CONJUNCTIONS

Name: _____

EXERCISE C: conjunctions in sentences   Accuracy _____ Creativity _____

Directions: Fill in the spaces with the appropriate grammatical units as directed.

1. _____ , nor
   (independent clause)

   _____ .
   (independent clause)

2. Both _____ and _____
   (proper noun)   *(proper noun)*

   _____ .
   (finish the sentence)

3. _____ ; consequently,
   (independent clause)

   _____ .
   (independent clause)

4. Even though _____ ,
   (finish the adverb clause)

   _____ .
   (independent clause)

5. On our vacation we not only _____ but also
   (transitive verb + direct object)

   _____ .
   (transitive verb + direct object)

6. _____ either by
   (independent clause)

   _____ or by _____
   (gerund phrase)   *(gerund phrase)*

   _____ .

7. Whenever _____ ,
    (finish the adverb clause)

    _____ .
    (independent clause)

8. The government official announced both that _____
    (finish the noun clause)

    _____

    and that _____ .
    (finish the noun clause)

9. _____ and _____
    (independent clause)   *(independent clause)*

    _____ , but _____ .
                                                        (independent clause)

10. Whether you _____ or you
    (finish the adverb clause)

    _____ , you will have to
    (finish the adverb clause)

    save up a lot of money.

7. PRONOUNS

A **pronoun** is a word that takes the place of a noun. It may replace any kind of noun, from a common noun to a noun clause. Here are some pairs of sentences that show how the substitution works.

(common noun)	*My mother* called. *Who* called?
(proper noun)	I wanted *a Coke*. I wanted *something*.
(infinitive phrase)	*To parasail in the Bahamas* was scary. *It* was scary.
(gerund phrase)	We loved *hiking the old logging trail*. We loved *that*.
(noun clause)	I'll choose *whoever works the hardest*. I'll choose *someone*.

1. **Interrogative pronouns:** The interrogative pronouns are *what, which, who,* and *whom.* These are pronouns we use to ask a question (interrogate) so that we can get a noun answer.

What do you have in your hand?	I have *a cricket* in my hand.
Who was at the game?	*Sister Catherine* was at the game.

Which is the best flavor?	*Rocky Road* is the best flavor.
Whom have you told?	I have told *my sister and her friend*.

2. **Demonstrative pronouns:** There are only four demonstrative pronouns, *this, that, these,* and *those*. These are used to "demonstrate" or point out a noun that is found elsewhere in the sentence or that is otherwise understood (notice the first word in this sentence).

These are very juicy peaches.
That is a wonderful idea.

Of all the songs on the album, I like *this* the best.

Note: Be able to distinguish the demonstrative pronouns from adjectives. Pronouns replace nouns; adjectives modify nouns. Compare:

That is a wonderful idea.	**demonstrative pronoun, replacing a noun**
That idea is wonderful.	**adjective, modifying a noun**

3. **Relative pronouns:** The relative pronouns are *who, whose, whom, which,* and *that*. You are already familiar with these pronouns, for they are what we used to construct the adjective clause.

Mr. Hanson, *who lives across the street,* hates kids.

That sentence was made from two sentences. We replaced *Mr. Hanson* in the second sentence with the pronoun *who* so that we could "relate" it to the first sentence.

Mr. Hanson hates kids.	~~Mr. Hanson~~ *who* lives across the street.

4.   **Intensive and reflexive pronouns:** These are the pronouns that end in -*self* or -*selves*. The **intensive pronoun** is used to intensify or emphasize a previously mentioned noun or pronoun.

> Mary *herself* was the last one to learn that she had won.

I spoke to the principal *himself* about the incident yesterday on the football field.

The **reflexive pronoun**, like a reflection in a mirror, refers back to the subject of the sentence.

> *I* hurt *myself* when I jumped off the swing.

Suddenly *they* found *themselves* stranded and sinking fast.

Reflexive pronouns must not be used instead of nominative or objective case pronouns.

Incorrect:	You can buy raffle tickets from Helen or myself.
Correct:	You can buy raffle tickets from Helen or *me*.
Incorrect:	Only two people, James and myself, knew the combination.
Correct:	Only two people, James and *I*, knew the combination.

5.   **Personal pronouns:** There are three cases in English: nominative, possessive, and objective.

The **possessive case** rarely causes trouble. We easily say *my* foot, *his* jacket, *her* schedule, *their* house, *whose* book bag. The only problem may occur with the *its* form. It must not be confused with *it's,* which is a contraction for *it is*. And it's (!) easy to remember; its (!) spelling is just like several other possessive pronouns, without an apostrophe: *yours, his, hers, its, ours, theirs.*

Nominative case:	*I*	*you*	*he*	*she*	*it*	*we*	*you*	*they*	*who*
Objective case:	*me*	*you*	*him*	*her*	*it*	*us*	*you*	*them*	*whom*

The **nominative case** of the pronoun is used when it is the subject of the sentence, when it follows a linking verb as a predicate nominative, or when it is in apposition to a noun being used as a subject or predicate nominative.

subject	Neither *she* nor *I* could find the car keys.
subject	*Who* answered the phone?
predicate nominative	My heroes are *they* who set high personal standards.
predicate nominative	We all knew that the talent contest winner would be *she*.
appositive	Only two girls, Jean and *I*, showed up for auditions.
appositive	They are such polite young men, both *he* and his brother.

The **objective case** of the pronoun is used when it is the direct object, the indirect object, or the object of a preposition, or it is in apposition to a noun being used as an object.

direct object	My mother found *them* in the closet.
direct object	*Whom* have you invited to the dance?
indirect object	She brought *me* my breakfast in bed.
indirect object	We showed *them* how to wind surf.
object of the preposition	Everyone except *me* was able to go to the auction.
object of the preposition	There were three people in the car, in addition to *him*.
object of the preposition	I didn't know by *whom* the letter was written.
appositive	I asked everyone, *her* and all her friends, but no one knew.
appositive	He received wild applause from everyone, especially *me*.

6. **Indefinite pronouns**: These are pronouns such as *anyone, somebody, none,* and *most.* Because the issue involving indefinite pronouns is agreement, not case, they will be covered in Chapter 9, "Agreement."

PRONOUN CASE ISSUES

Case in speaking and writing: It is important to remember that there is a difference between spoken and written language. On the telephone a "That's me" is quite acceptable, but in formal writing the predicate nominative form of the pronoun is required after a linking verb.

Correct: Did they know that *it was I* who first called the police?

A much less acceptable speech pattern has recently become common, using the objective case pronoun in the subject position. It occurs almost exclusively when there are two subjects.

Incorrect: Me and him want to go with you.

Such a blunder should find no place in any of your speaking or writing. The correct form can usually be determined by taking the items one at a time.

He wants to go with you.	*I* want to go with you.	**Correct:**	*He and I* want to go with you.

A similar situation arises with the use of *we* or *us* used to emphasize or clarify a noun. The correct case of the pronoun may be determined simply by omitting the noun.

We / Us ~~novices~~ didn't stand a chance.	= *We* didn't stand a chance.
I hope she appreciates we / us ~~volunteers~~.	= I hope she appreciates *us*.

Here are some more challenging situations. Circle the correct pronouns. Any other changes?

Should he/him and I/me leave now?	No one but we/us tenors were singing.
It's easy for they/them and we/us.	The ones who know best are we/us students.

The only preposition inappropriate for such a strategy of taking one pronoun at a time is *between,* which of necessity must be followed by two objects. Imagine, therefore, that the preposition is *with.*

Problem:	It was a secret between he/him and I/me.
	It was a secret with *him*.
	It was a secret with *me*.
Solution:	It was a secret between *him* and *me*.

Case in comparisons: Comparisons involving pronouns must also be watched carefully. Sometimes words are implied but not written. Most often, these comparisons involve the use of the subordinating conjunctions *than* or *as ... as.* You can determine the correct case for the pronoun by supplying the missing words.

I like Cynthia better than *she* (does).
I like Cynthia better than (I like) *her*.
You don't know David as well as *I* (do).
You don't know David as well as (you know) *me*.

OTHER PRONOUN ISSUES

Ambiguous or vague pronoun reference: There are other pronoun difficulties besides determining the correct case. You know that a pronoun takes the place of a noun or another pronoun. That *antecedent* must be clear to the reader. A misunderstood pronoun could cause confusion, amusement, or anger. Such errors can usually be corrected by the use of a noun instead of the pronoun, a rearrangement of word order, or a direct quotation.

Ambiguous:	When the boys brought home the fish they had caught, Dad cleaned them.
Correct:	When the boys brought home the fish they had caught, Dad cleaned the fish.

Ambiguous:	I put the car in the garage and locked it.
Correct:	I locked the car after I put it in the garage.
	I locked the garage after I put the car in.

Ambiguous:	Jack told Ed that he had broken his favorite putter.
Correct:	Jack told Ed, "I have broken your favorite putter."
	Jack told Ed, "I have broken my favorite putter."
	Jack told Ed, "You have broken your favorite putter."
	Jack told Ed, "You have broken my favorite putter."

Vague:	Tracy is always thinking about her brother's computer, which keeps her from getting her work done.
Correct:	Tracy's constant thinking about her brother's computer keeps her from getting her work done.
	Tracy is always thinking about her brother's computer, whose silly beeping keeps her from getting her work done.

You learned In Chapter 3, "Adjectives" (page 51), that the antecedent of a relative pronoun may be an entire sentence.

I bought the first pair of shoes I tried on, *which proved to be a mistake*.

However, such a construction may result in an ambiguous pronoun reference if the antecedent is not clear.

I saw *Romeo and Juliet* in London, which was fabulous.

What was fabulous? The play? London? Seeing the play in London? In a situation like this, rewrite the sentence so that there is no question about its meaning.

I saw a fabulous production of *Romeo and Juliet* in London.

I saw *Romeo and Juliet* in London, which is a fabulous city.

Seeing *Romeo and Juliet* in London was fabulous.

PRONOUNS

Name: _____

EXERCISE A: pronoun case

Accuracy _____

Directions: In the spaces below, insert the correct forms of *I/me, he/him, she/her, we/us, they/them,* or *who/whom.* Do not use *you* or *it,* because they are the same in both the nominative and objective case and hence pose no problem. On the line below each sentence, explain why you chose that case.

Examples: Does either *he* or his dad have a tire pump I can borrow?
_____ Subject of *Does* _____
The ball flew right between *her and me*.
_____ Objects of preposition *between* _____

There is at least one sentence that could be completed by using either the nominative or objective case pronoun. Which one? Be prepared to explain the difference between the two choices.

1. We appreciated her talent more than _____ .

    _____

2. Give the envelope to the first person _____ gets here.

    _____

3. David and _____ camped out last night.

    _____

4. Suddenly through the choppy water came _____ and his father.

    _____

5. Is this director better than _____ ?

    _____

6. I couldn't figure out to _____ her remarks were directed.

    _____

7. There were no secrets between my uncle and _____.

    _____

8. Anyone as old as _____ should know better.

    _____

9. Was it _____ who sent the letter?

    _____

83

10. I trust no one as much as _____.

_____

11. I said I would meet Ruth and _____ at noon.

_____

12. All except _____ were chosen.

_____

13. I can invite only one person, either you or _____ .

_____

14. No one can put up a tent as fast as _____ .

_____

15. The train conductor told _____ where to put our luggage.

_____

16. Is this the man _____ helped you get home?

_____

17. We determined that the prank caller could not have been _____ .

_____

18. No one besides _____ knew the combination to the safe.

_____

19. Suddenly the teacher asked _____ a question.

_____

20. I had to decide by Friday _____ I wanted as my lab partner.

_____

PRONOUNS

Name: _____

EXERCISE B: pronoun reference

Accuracy _____

Directions: All the sentences below have ambiguous or vague pronoun references. For each, rewrite the entire sentence so that it reads correctly.

1. Dr. Payne told Dr. Graves that he would have to operate.

   _____

2. I went sledding on Saturday with my new sled, which was wonderful.

   _____

3. My little brother let the dog out and then he started howling.

   _____

4. Before you cut the wallpaper for the bathroom, measure it.

   _____

5. Many teachers have computers in their classrooms, and the students love them.

   _____

6. If the passenger air bag is not included in the car's price, you should not buy it.

   _____

7. The tire on her bike was blown and the chain had fallen off, but most of it was repairable.

   _____

8. After seeing the lion tamer's assistant, I decided that I wanted to be one.

   _____

9. My mother used to read me all the Dr. Seuss stories, which I loved.

   _____

10. I have studied German for three years, and I hope to visit it next year.

   _____

11. I asked my father to get Mr. Sandler's recipe for chocolate chip cookies because he is such a good cook.

_____

_____

12. Before we let the children play with the old clothes from the attic, we will have to wash them.

_____

13. I went on the Ferris wheel, won a stuffed giraffe at the darts booth, and ate a huge soft pretzel with mustard; it was wonderful.

_____

_____

14. Topher asked Zach why nobody liked him.

_____

15. The disk drive on my computer is broken, but I can't afford a new one.

_____

16. The dessert was a hot fudge sundae with a cherry on top. That was the best part of the meal.

_____

17. We painted a scar on the face of the scarecrow, but it still didn't look very scary.

_____

18. Charlene noticed that the store clerk was nervous as she approached.

_____

19. I tried to attach the bracket with my cordless screwdriver, but it didn't work.

_____

20. Before I could introduce Mrs. Giordano to my sister, she had left.

_____

8. THE ABSOLUTE PHRASE

We devote now an entire chapter to a grammatical construction that is a favorite with many writers but does not conform to the guidelines for any of the phrases or clauses we have considered so far. It is called the **absolute phrase,** and it is probably the single most important element you can learn to improve your writing.

The absolute phrase is a group of words that is set off from the main clause, usually by commas, but which helps to develop the actions, characters, or ideas established in the main clause. It is made by removing the finite verb (usually *was* or *were)* from a sentence. The resulting absolute phrase thus consists of a subject and the remainder of the original predicate. Here is how the transformation occurs.

Main clause:	She held the boa constrictor carefully.
Sentence to be added:	Its skin was surprisingly smooth and dry.
Remove the finite verb:	*was*
Resulting absolute phrase:	its skin surprisingly smooth and dry
Final sentence:	She held the boa constrictor carefully, *its skin surprisingly smooth and dry.*

Main clause:	The pole vaulter rose over the crossbar.
Sentence to be added:	His legs were kicking toward the sky.
Remove the finite verb:	*were*
Resulting absolute phrase:	his legs kicking toward the sky
Final sentence:	The pole vaulter rose over the crossbar, *his legs kicking toward the sky.*

The predicate of an absolute phrase may be any of the grammatical constructions that regularly follow *was* or *were* in a sentence. Below, the absolute phrase in each sentence is in *italics.* Determine what the subject is, and then observe how the grammatical construction indicated is being used as the predicate of the absolute phrase. Also try mentally putting *was* or *were* back into the absolute phrase.

Present participle:	He stood there, *his hand shielding his eyes from the sun.*
Past participle:	The radio-controlled airplane lay quietly on the ground, *its wings broken from the sudden impact.*
Infinitive:	The prisoner looked around frantically, *his only hope to jump onto the approaching train.*
Noun:	The actress read her lines, *her voice hardly a whisper.*
Pronoun:	The campground was quiet, *the only sounds those of the crickets and jumping fish.*
Adjective:	She kicked at the back door, *her hands full of groceries.*
Adverb:	The gym teacher assumed the first position, *her arms out in front of her.*
Prep. phrase:	He entered the bank, *a gun in each hand and a ski mask over his head.*
Comparison:	He closed his eyes and got ready for his first kiss, *his puckered lips like those of a hungry goldfish.*

With as a marker of the absolute phrase: Sometimes an absolute phrase will begin with the word *with*. It should not be confused with a prepositional phrase. In a prepositional phrase, removing the *with* would destroy the phrase. But here, removing the *with* still leaves an absolute phrase.

> The tall ship glided into the harbor, *with its sails bulging majestically.*

Which of the examples on the previous page could begin with *with*? Which do you think is better?

Sometimes an absolute phrase will begin a sentence. Such positioning is especially useful when you want your reader to know immediately either why or how the main action occurred.

> *With the rain starting to fall*, we headed toward the shore.
> *Her hands folded in her lap*, she offered the Thanksgiving prayer.

Notice in the second example that the word *folded* is the past participle form of the verb (her hands *were folded*) and not the past tense of the verb. In English, both the past and the past participle forms of regular verbs end with *–ed*. You must make sure you are using the proper form, or you will end up with run-on sentences. Test your absolute phrase by inserting the helping verb *was* or *were* in front of the *–ed* verb form. If it now reads as a logical sentence, your absolute phrase is correct.

THE ABSOLUTE PHRASE: SAMPLES

She thundered down the seawall road, *arms held out behind her like the silver lady on a Rolls Royce, steam snorting from her wide nostrils.*
— John Varley, *Wizard*

Up through the dim pine trees they went, *the constable's breath wheezing in her ears.*
— Natalie Babbit, *Tuck Everlasting*

Rosamunde looked like always, in a big blue windbreaker with PAL on it, in denim overalls that did nothing for her figure, *her brown hair thick and curly in two ponytails at the sides of her head, her face all wrinkled up around her beady eyes,* the way it got when she was thinking hard.
— Cynthia Voigt, *Izzy, Willy Nilly*

With scarcely a word said, four of us, the chauffeur, butler, gardener, and I, hurried down to the pool.
— F. Scott Fitzgerald, *The Great Gatsby*

There was a black-haired girl with the same blue eyes, and her hair hung long and she was dressed all in black, *with a girdle of silver about her waist.*
— Roger Zelazny, *The Chronicles of Amber, Vol. 1*

"Don't tell me you are going to send me away!" exclaimed Oliver, *the tone of his voice alarmed and serious.*
— Charles Dickens, *Oliver Twist*

A beautiful job, *his hair combed, his tie straight, the light hitting his eyes just right to make them glisten.*
— William Kittredge and Steven Krauzer, *The Great American Detective*

They set off again, *the hunters bunched a little by fear of the mentioned beast,* while Jack quested ahead.
— William Golding, *Lord of the Flies*

THE ABSOLUTE PHRASE

Name: _____

EXERCISE A: writing absolute phrase predicates

Accuracy _____ Creativity _____

Directions: In the sentences below, the subject for an absolute phrase has been provided. Complete the phrases with predicates as directed.

1. She played the guitar solo with confidence, her fingers _____
   (present participle as predicate)

   _____ .

2. On the count of three we all jumped into the water, our arms _____
   (past participle as predicate)

   _____ .

3. Everyone had arrived for dress rehearsal by six o'clock, the actors _____
   (infinitive as predicate)

   _____ , the stage hands _____
   (infinitive as predicate)

   _____ , and the director _____
   (infinitive as predicate)

   _____ .

4. The antique roll-top desk was my family's most treasured heirloom, its many compartments

   _____ , and its golden oak finish
   (noun as predicate)

   _____ .
   (noun as predicate)

5. The movie billed as the "laugh hit of the summer" was a big disappointment, with jokes so _____

   _____ .
   (adjective as predicate)

6. She looked like a Parisian model, her dress _____
   (pronoun as predicate)

   _____ .

7. He stood at attention in front of the colonel, his eyes _____

   (adverb as predicate)

   _____ .

8. The table was set for the banquet, with the food _____

   (prepositional phrase as predicate)

   _____ .

9. At the end of the race he was exhausted, his legs _____

   (comparison as predicate)

   _____ .

10. She looked into the dark room, her eyes _____

    (any kind of predicate)

    _____ .

THE ABSOLUTE PHRASE

Name: _____

EXERCISE B: writing absolute phrases   Accuracy _____ Creativity _____

Directions: In each space below, write a complete absolute phrase that develops the idea established in the independent clause. Write both the subject and the predicate as directed.

1.   At last we arrived at the cabin, _____ _____
     (subject)   *(present participle as predicate)*

     _____ .

2.   With _____ _____
          (subject)   *(past participle as predicate)*

     _____ , the graduates crossed the stage.

3.   The matador, _____ _____
                    (subject)   *(present participle as predicate)*

     _____ , slowly approached the motionless bull.

4.   The dogs sniffed their way along the trail, _____ _____
                                                  (subject)   *(adverb as predicate)*

     _____ and _____
                                             (subject)

     _____ .
     (adjective as predicate)

5.   With _____ _____
          (subject)   *(past participle as predicate)*

     _____ , the sky diver pushed off into oblivion.

6.   We divided the car wash crew into two groups, _____ _____
                                                    (subject)   *(infinitive as predicate)*

     _____ and _____
                                             (subject)

     _____ .
     (infinitive as predicate)

7. His history essay left much to be desired, _____ _____
   (subject)   (noun as predicate)

   _____ and _____
   (subject)

   _____ .
   (noun as predicate)

8. With _____ _____
   (subject)   (present participle as predicate)

   _____ , my dog easily won "Best of Show."

9. With _____ _____ and
   (subject)   (adjective as predicate)

   _____ _____ , the jungle was virtually impassable.
   (subject)   (adjective as predicate)

10. With only seconds remaining, he wrestled his opponent furiously, _____
    (subject)

    _____ _____ .
    (present participle as predicate)   (comparison)

EXERCISE c: reading for absolute phrases

Accuracy _____

Directions: Read in a good book and find three sentences containing absolute phrases. Write the sentences below. This works best with fiction describing scenes of adventure. Also tell the book's title and author.

_____

_____

_____

_____

_____

_____

Title and Author: _____

9. AGREEMENT

SUBJECT AND VERB AGREEMENT

The verb in a sentence must be singular if the subject is singular and plural if the subject is plural. In other words, the subject and verb must *agree in number*.

Although this sounds like an easy rule to follow, problems of agreement can arise for a number of reasons.

Intervening words: Sometimes there are words between the subject and the verb that make us lose track of what the real subject of the sentence is.

> The *collection* of Chinese porcelain vases *has* been stolen.

> *My sister*, together with both her roommates, *was* selected to be on the planning committee.

Sometimes the intervening phrase will begin with *accompanied by, along with, as well as*, or *in addition to*. Such phrases must be recognized as modifiers, and they do not change a singular subject to a plural.

Correlative conjunctions: In the "Conjunctions" chapter we pointed out that the correlative conjunctions *either... or* and *neither... nor* sometimes give difficulty. But there is a simple rule to follow. Look at the noun or pronoun that is closer to the *inflected* verb. Singular makes it singular; plural makes it plural.

> Neither the president nor the *treasurer was* able to explain the budget.

> Neither the president nor his *advisors were* able to explain the budget.

> *Does* either your *mother* or your father have a ticket?

> *Do* either your *parents* or your brother have tickets?

There **and** *here:* The words *there* and *here* may begin sentences and delay the subject until after the verb. Also, in speech they are often combined with the verb to form a contraction, especially *there's* and *here's*. Make sure you can identify the subject in such a sentence, and make the verb agree.

> There *was* no *reason* to think that we would fail.

> There *were*, by the time the game started, at least two thousand *people* in the stands.

> Here in my knapsack *is everything* that I need for my bicycle trip in the Rockies.

> Here *are* the *tools* that you sent me for.

One of: A common sentence pattern involves the phrase *one of those, one of these*, or *one of the*, followed by a plural noun and an adjective clause. In most cases the verb of the adjective clause will be plural, because the antecedent of the relative pronoun is the plural noun before the clause

Carl is	+	one of those	+	[*athletes* who *train* hard.]
I bought	+	one of those	+	[*hats* that *have* earflaps inside.]

The only exception to this rule occurs if the phrase is preceded by *the only*. Now the antecedent of the relative pronoun is singular, so the verb must be singular.

She is	+	[*the only one*]	+	of the athletes	+	[*who was* named all-state.]
I'm buying	+	[*the only one*]	+	of the hats	+	[*that matches* my mittens.]

Remember, too, that in sentences such as these there may also be pronouns that must be consistent with the number of the noun.

Clyde is one of those *students* who never *seem* to get *their* homework in on time.

Cynthia is *the only girl* I know who *works* on *her* own car.

Amount and number: Expressions concerning an amount will be singular, and expressions concerning a number greater than one will be plural.

Twenty dollars was too much to pay for the dinner. (an amount of money)

Twenty balloons were given out to the first twenty children. (a number of balloons)

Four weeks was a long time to spend alone at sea. (an amount of time)

Four months do not contain the letter *r*. (a number of months)

The word *number* itself as the subject of the sentence may be singular or plural. Generally, *the number* will be singular and *a number* will be plural.

The number of people suffering from opioid addiction *is* rising.

A number of people *have* not filled out the questionnaire.

Fractions and percentages may also refer to an amount or a number.

Three quarters of an hour *is* all that we have left. (an amount of time)

Two thirds of the pizza *has* mushrooms and onions. (an amount of pizza)

Eighty per cent of the new highway *has* been completed. (amount of highway)

Nine tenths of the students *were* in favor of the proposal. (a number of students)

Three fourths of the games *were* won by Indiana State. (a number of games)

Over *ninety per cent* of the graduates *go* on to college. (a number of graduates)

As you see by these examples, fractions and percentages will usually be followed by a prepositional phrase beginning with *of,* and the object of the preposition will signal you whether the verb should be singular or plural.

Nouns joined by *and* but singular: Sometimes you will want to refer to a single noun by using two or more nouns joined by *and*. Since together they represent a single subject, the verb will be singular.

His teacher, advisor, coach, and confidant *is* none other than his father.

Where I bought it and how much I paid for it *is* my business.

AGREEMENT

Name: _____

EXERCISE A: subject and verb agreement   Accuracy _____ Creativity _____

Directions: Fill in the spaces below as directed. Sometimes you may choose either of the suggested verbs, depending on your subject. Other times, only one of the suggested verbs is possible. There are also some sentences in which the verb is provided. Make sure that the subject you write agrees with that verb. Do not use a proper noun in any of the subject positions.

1.   There _____ _____ in the trunk of the car.
          (is/are)   *(subject)*

2.   _____ _____ too much to pay.
     (amount of money)   *(was/were)*

3.   She is one of those _____ who _____ every day.
                              (plural noun)   *(verb in the present tense)*

4.   The only thing _____
                              (intervening words)

     _____ _____ his voice.
                                                              (was/were)

5.   My favorite _____ , and the one
                              (singular noun)

     _____ , is
          (adjective clause)

     _____ .
          (complete the sentence)

6.   Neither _____ nor _____ _____ to go.
          (singular subject)   *(plural subject)*   *(has/have)*

7.   Neither _____ nor _____ _____ left.
          (plural subject)   *(singular subject)*   *(has/have)*

8.   Does either _____ or _____
                    (subject)   *(subject)*

     _____ know how to operate the remote control?

9.   One third of the _____ _____
                              (singular noun)   *(was/were)*

     _____ .
          (complete the sentence)

10. Here are _____
          (complete the sentence)

     _____ .

11. His _____ , as well as _____
    (singular subject)   (intervening phrase with plural noun)

    _____ , _____ been missing since Saturday.
                                           (has/have)

12. _____ number of _____
    (A/The)   (complete the phrase)

    _____ _____ incorrect.
                                                (is/are)

13. Half of the _____
    (plural noun)

    _____ _____ .
    (was/were)   (complete the sentence)

14. My aunt is one of those _____ who _____
    (plural noun)   (is/are)

    _____ .
    (complete the sentence using **her** or **their**)

15. My sister is the only one of the _____ who
    (plural noun)

    _____ .
    (complete the sentence using **has** or **have**)

16. _____ of the _____
    (a percentage)   (either singular or plural noun)

    _____ _____ .
    (was/were)   (complete the sentence)

17. My _____ and _____
    (singular subject)   (singular subject)

    has always been _____ .
                     (complete the sentence)

18. _____ , in addition to me and all of my elementary school friends, _____
    (singular subject)   (was/were)

    _____ .
    (complete the sentence)

19. There _____ _____ .
    (was/were)   (complete the sentence)

20. Have either _____ or
    (subject, not a proper noun)

    _____ ever been to Chinatown in San Francisco?
    (subject, not a proper noun)

PRONOUN AGREEMENT

In Chapter 7 on pronouns (page 81) you learned that there are many kinds of pronouns, and that with personal pronouns you have to be careful about case.

There is one more category of pronoun that we have saved for this chapter, because these pronouns often present difficulties with agreement. These are the **indefinite pronouns.** There are three categories of indefinite pronouns:

always singular:	*everybody, everyone, everything, anybody, anyone, anything, somebody, someone, something, nobody, no one, nothing, each, either, neither, one*

Neither of his proposals *was* acceptable.

Does everyone understand the problem?

always plural:	*both, few, many, several*

Few know the real reason he quit.

Many have been known to get lost in this desert.

singular or plural:	*all, any, most, none, some*

These indefinite pronouns can go either way. Usually they are followed by a prepositional phrase beginning with *of,* or such a prepositional phrase is implied. If the object of the preposition is singular, then the verb is singular; if the object of the preposition is plural, the verb is plural.

Some of the *milk was* spilled.

Some of the milk *bottles were* broken.

None of her *writing was* legible.

None of her *papers were* acceptable.

The difficulties involving indefinite pronouns are often multiplied because it is not just the verb that must be considered. There might be other pronouns in the sentence that have to agree with their pronoun antecedent.

No one who *doesn't* get *his* application in on time *is* going to be considered.

Many of my friends inherited *their* political preferences from *their* parents.

As may be seen by the first example, the use of the singular pronoun may lead to misunderstandings or injustices regarding gender. What about the girls who are submitting applications?

One remedy is to make all the singular pronoun references apply to both sexes by writing both the pronouns *(he and she, his and hers, him and her).* Such a construction is acceptable on a limited basis, but with repeated use becomes self-conscious and distracting from the writing itself. Therefore, it should be used with restraint.

Another remedy, common in spoken and informal written English, is to shift into the plural pronoun.

> If *anyone* calls, tell *them* I'll be back around noon.

The technical term for this shift is *synesis*. Our concern in this book, however, is with the standards of formal written English, and there are other effective ways to avoid these pronoun dilemmas.

The first alternative is to make everything plural. Our first example above would thus become

> *People* who *don't* get *their* applications in on time *are* not going to be considered.

The other alternative is to circumvent the problem altogether by rewriting the sentence without pronoun references. For the above sentence, you might write

> Only applications submitted on time will be considered.

And finally, the appropriate pronoun may be determined by the meaning of the sentence rather than by the rules of agreement. Compare the clear differences in meaning of these sentences:

> Neither Bill nor his sister could do *his* math homework.
> Neither Bill nor his sister could do *her* math homework.
> Neither Bill nor his sister could do *their* math homework.

When faced with writing challenges such as these, make sure that the grammar you use is appropriate for your writing situation and that it expresses your meaning clearly and correctly.

AGREEMENT

Name: _____

EXERCISE B: agreement of all kinds

Accuracy _____

Directions: Fill in each blank with the correct form of the verb, noun, or pronoun, either singular or plural. Some may have more than one possible answer. Be prepared to discuss your choice.

1. Several of the jigsaw pieces, along with the cover of the box, _____ lost.
    (was) (were)

2. _____ some of the pages in this book appear newer than others to you?
    (Does) (Do)

3. Each of the brochures she has received from the colleges _____ more enticing
    (looks) (look)

    than the one before it.

4. Few of the rides at the Fourth of July carnival this year _____ worth the price of admission.
    (was) (were)

5. When everybody arrives, tell _____ that _____
    (him) (him or her) (them)   *(he) (he or she) (they)*

    should make _____ at home.
    (himself) (himself or herself) (themselves)

6. _____ all of this year's supply of chalk been used up already?
    (Has) (Have)

7. None of the reasons offered by the girl for her lateness _____ acceptable.
    (was) (were)

8. Did either the conductor or the members of the orchestra ever find _____ baton?
    (his) (their)

9. Almost all of the information compiled in 2010 by the Labor Department concerning population

    and jobs _____ become outdated.
    (has) (have)

10. Neither of the male leads in the play _____ been able to get _____
    (has) (have)   *(his) their)*

    _____ to stay in place.
    (beard) (beards)

11. He is one of the scientists who _____ working on magnetic levitation.
    (is) (are)

12. The number of latenesses you are allowed each semester _____ been exceeded.
    (has) (have)

13. _____ any of the stories in the collection written by Ray Bradbury?
    (Was) (Were)

14. Every one of the family's missing videotapes _____ found in the hall closet.
    (was) (were)

15. _____ either of the kittens been named yet?
    (Has) (Have)

16. I'd love one of those doughnuts that _____ Bavarian cream in _____ .
    (has) (have)   (it) (them)

17. Anyone who _____ _____ order in on time is sure to get the one
    (gets) (get)   (his) (his or her) (their)

    _____ _____ .
    (he) (he or she) (they)   (wants) (want)

18. Two thirds of the jury _____ never heard of a writ of habeas corpus.
    (has) (have)

19. This phone is the only one of the phones on sale that _____ one of those converters that
    (has) (have)

    _____ directly to the smart TV.
    (connects) (connect)

20. Both David and I had trouble getting _____ soap box racer to steer properly.
    (my) (his) (our)

10. USAGE

There are many words and phrases in English that present problems to even the best of writers. Sometimes there may be confusion over spelling (*complementary/complimentary, principal/ principle*); other times we are tempted to use the wrong part of speech (*bad/badly, good/well*); still other times similar words may have quite separate meanings that must be distinguished (*continually/ continuously, allusion/illusion*). Such issues fall under the heading **usage**, and we must learn how to *use* the word or phrase that is appropriate. Below is a summary of the most common usage problems, followed by exercises that will give you practice in writing the correct forms.

PART ONE

accept	*Accept* is a verb meaning "to approve" or "to receive."
	She *accepted* the applause with a simple wave of her hand. I cannot *accept* your explanation.
except	*Except* may be a verb meaning "to exclude" or "to make an exception," or it may be a preposition meaning "with the exception of."
	Seniors were *excepted* from study hall yesterday. Nobody *except* Carolyn remembers the quadratic formula.
adapt	*Adapt* means "to adjust" or "to make more suitable."
	It takes me at least two days to *adapt* to the different traffic rules when I drive in London.
adopt	*Adopt* means "to take as one's own."
	We finally *adopted* his suggestion to shorten the work week.
affect	*Affect* is a verb meaning "to influence," or "to move emotionally."
	His injury in the third quarter did not *affect* his play. I was quite *affected* by her account of her escape from Nazi Germany.
effect	*Effect* can be a verb or a noun. As a verb it means "to bring about."
	We could not *effect* the change in the graduation requirements without the approval of the Dean of Studies.
	As a noun it means "a result, outcome; also, a state of being in force."
	We don't yet know the side *effects* of this drug. That law is no longer in *effect*.
allusion	An *allusion* is an indirect reference. The verb form is *allude*.
	The candidate's *allusion* to the New Deal raised a few eyebrows.
illusion	An *illusion* is a mistaken perception of reality, or a misconception.
	The magician's levitation trick gave the *illusion* of weightlessness.

elude	Also be familiar with the verb *elude*, "to avoid being captured by."
	Despite his beard, shaved head, and fake limp, he could not *elude* the police dragnet.
alot	There is no such word. It is a misspelling of the article and noun *a lot*.
	There was *a lot* of interest in an all-school carnival.
allot	The verb *allot* means "to set aside as a portion or share."
	The troop leader *allotted* one candle and three matches to each scout.
alright	There is no such word. It is a misspelling of *all right*.
	Is it *all right* to call you by your first name?
among	*Among* and *between* are prepositions. The object of *among* denotes more than two things.
	The new substitution rule caused much confusion *among* the coaches in the league.
between	The object of *between* usually denotes only two things.
	The sibling rivalry *between* my sister and me was driving my mother wild.
	There are situations, however, when *between* is used with more than two nouns to show that the situation occurs in pairs, two at a time.
	The sibling rivalry *between* my older brother, my sister, and me was driving my mother wild.
awhile	*Awhile* is an adverb. Do not use it as the object of a preposition.
	After resting *awhile*, we resumed our climb to the summit.
a while	The expression *a while* may be used either by itself or as the object of a preposition (*for a while, in a while, after a while*).
	I wanted to stay in bed *a while* longer. After *a while*, the smoke cleared.
bad	*Bad* is an adjective and may follow a linking verb.
	It looked *bad* for the Mudville Nine that day. I felt *bad* about missing your wedding.
badly	*Badly* is an adverb and modifies an action verb or a past participle.
	I played *badly* in the doubles match. His *badly* torn parka was leaking feathers everywhere.
being as or **being that**	Neither of these expressions should begin a sentence. Use *since* or *because* instead. Since (or *because*) we were late, we had to sit in the balcony.

beside	*Beside* is a preposition meaning "next to."
	There was an oxygen tank *beside* his bed.
besides	*Besides* is either a preposition meaning "in addition to" or an adverb meaning "also" or "moreover."
	Besides his uncle, he has no living relatives. We had a dozen candles, three flashlights, two lanterns—and an electric generator *besides*!
complement **complementary**	*Complement* is a noun or verb based on the word *complete*. In grammar we have a subject complement after a linking verb. The adjective form is *complementary*. In geometry we speak of complementary angles, two angles that complete a right angle of 90°.
	This scarf is a nice *complement* to your outfit. George and Lenny's abilities were *complementary*.
compliment **complimentary**	A *compliment* is a noun or verb referring to praise, or something freely given. The adjective form is *complimentary*.
	My English teacher *complimented* me on my writing style. Here is a *complimentary* pair of tickets to the symphony.
continual **continually**	*Continual* or *continually* indicates that an action occurs many times in succession, but with breaks.
	He was *continually* raising his hand during the lecture.
continuous **continuously**	*Continuous* or *continuously* indicates that an action occurs over a period of time, without interruption.
	The alarm rang *continuously* until the store owner arrived.
council	A council is a group of people, often elected, who discuss and advise on issues. A member of such a group, especially in local government, is called a *councilor*.
	The student *council* meets every Tuesday after lunch.
counsel	*Counsel* means "advice or guidance," and the person who gives it is a *counselor*. It may also be used as a verb. Sometimes an attorney is referred to as "legal counsel."
	Since she was an alumna of my first-choice college, I asked her for *counsel*. He needs someone to *counsel* him about his drinking problem.
consul	This is an officer in the foreign service of a government. A consul works in a *consulate*.
	I met the chief *consul* from Venezuela at the international dinner.

credible	*Credible* means "believable," as opposed to *incredible*.
	It certainly was unusual, but your explanation is *credible.*
creditable	*Creditable* means "worthy of praise."
	They were only amateurs, but they gave a *creditable* performance.
credulous	*Credulous* means "gullible; believing just about anything."
	I knew by the *credulous* look on his face that he was believing my silly story.
different from	*From* is a preposition, so *different from* should be followed by a noun or pronoun as the object of that preposition. Be aware that the sentence may continue with an adjective clause, however.
	Why is your answer *different from* mine? This color is *different from* the one that we ordered.
different than	*Than* is a subordinating conjunction, so *different than* should be followed immediately by an adverb clause.
	The outcome of the election was *different than* we had hoped.
disinterested	*Disinterested* means "impartial, having no personal interest or stake in the matter."
	It was hard to find twelve *disinterested* townspeople for the jury.
uninterested	*Uninterested* means "indifferent, not caring."
	She wanted me to go to the fundraiser, but I was *uninterested* in their cause.
emigrate **emigrant**	*Emigrate* (based on *ex*, "out") means to leave one's country and settle in another. It is usually followed by *from* and the place of departure.
	Many farmers *emigrated* from Ireland during the potato famine.
immigrate **immigrant**	*Immigrate* (based on *in*, "in") means to come into a country to settle. It is usually followed by *to* and the place of arrival.
	My great grandparents *immigrated* to the United States from Armenia in 1911.
eminent	*Eminent* means "distinguished."
	An *eminent* theologian delivered the invocation.
imminent	*Imminent* means "about to occur" or "threatening."
	The divers on the reef were in *imminent* danger.
explicit	*Explicit* means "expressed directly."
	The warranty was *explicit*: thirty days or one thousand miles.
implicit	*Implicit* means "implied or expressed indirectly."
	Our relationship was based on *implicit* trust.

USAGE

Name: _____

EXERCISE A: part one — usage editing

Accuracy _____

Directions: All of the sentences below contain at least one error in usage that was covered in Part One. Draw a line through any word that is not used correctly, and put the correct form beneath it in the space provided.

Example: The president of the Student ~~Counsel~~ made an ~~illusion~~ to Patrick Henry.
Council *allusion*

1. I am continuously having to give implicit directions to the emigrants to make them understand.

_____

2. Alot of people feel badly when they forget to compliment the host after a successful party.

_____

3. Being that she is an imminent geneticist, we should probably consider her theory credible.

_____

4. Did my continual interruptions effect your concentration very bad?

_____

5. Everything will be alright for awhile if we make up a creditable story to tell the counselor.

_____

6. The new light switch was different than the old one, but we were able to adopt it easily.

_____

7. I have no allusions about how much my counsel can affect the result you desire so bad.

_____

8. Beside its wanting continuous sunlight, there is no difference between this plant and the others.

_____

9. The affect of the drug on the patient was different from what the eminent doctors had expected.

_____

10. My credulous older sister will accept any complement as an implicit proposal of marriage.

_____

USAGE

Name: _____

EXERCISE B: part one — usage writing   **Accuracy** _____ **Creativity** _____

Directions: In the spaces below, write sentences that illustrate the correct usage of the words and phrases indicated. Each sentence contains two usage issues, and you may add others if you wish. You do not have to use them in the order given, and you may use whatever form that is appropriate and correct (singular/plural, noun/adjective/adverb, past/present/future tense). Try to write sentences both that are creative and that reinforce and clarify the correct usage of the given words. "I was uninterested and credulous" does little to address the usage problems.

1. (continual; except) _____

    _____

2. (adopt; affect) _____

    _____

3. (credible; awhile) _____

    _____

4. (explicit; eminent) _____

    _____

5. (immigrate; different from) _____

    _____

6. (emigrant; different than) _____

    _____

7. (among; allusion) _____

    _____

8. (bad [as predicate adjective]; between) _____

    _____

9. (complement; implicit) _____

    _____

10. (effect; credulous) _____ _____

_____

11. (disinterested; continuous) _____

_____

12. (counselor; immigrant) _____

_____

13. (uninterested; illusion) _____

_____

14. (emigrant; creditable) _____

_____

15. (besides; among) _____

_____

16. (accept; adapt) _____

_____

17. (a lot; imminent) _____

_____

18. (compliment; consul) _____

_____

19. (council; effect) _____

_____

20. (beside; a while) _____

_____

PART TWO

farther	*Farther* is the comparative form of *far* and is used when referring to physical distance.
	I have never run *farther* than a mile in my whole life.
further	*Further* means "to a greater distance in degree or time," "to a greater extent," or "additional."
	I refuse to discuss the matter *further*.
	There will be no *further* assignments in this book.
fewer	*Fewer* should be used when referring to a number of items, things that can be counted.
	There are *fewer* students in the Government class this year.
less	*Less* should be used when referring to an amount, including time and money.
	There was *less* frosting on my cake than on hers.
	Anyone who has lived here *less* than ten years is considered "new."
	So the sign at the checkout line in the grocery store should read "Ten items or..."
hanged	*Hanged* is the past tense of the verb *hang* when referring to death by hanging. The past participle form may be either *hanged* or *hung*.
	In *The Ox-Bow Incident,* the mob hanged the wrong men.
hardly or **scarcely**	*Hardly* or *scarcely*, when combined with words such as *not, nothing,* or *without,* create an unacceptable double negative.
	Incorrect: We couldn't hardly afford bus fare when we were first married.
	Correct: We *could hardly* afford bus fare when we were first married.
	Incorrect: Without scarcely a sound, we opened the door to the cellar.
	Correct: With *scarcely* a sound, we opened the door to the cellar.
imply	*Imply* means "to express indirectly; suggest." The noun form is *implication*.
	I did not mean to *imply* that your help was not appreciated.
infer	*Infer* means "to conclude by reasoning; deduce." The noun form is *inference*.
	I *inferred* from your remark that you wanted to quit your job.
irregardless	There is no such word. The correct word is *regardless,* meaning "heedless" or "in spite of everything."
	She continued to snap her gum, *regardless* of the others in the theater.
	I know you've been sick for four days and didn't have your books at home. *Regardless,* you'll have to take the test today.

...is when **...is where** **...is because**	These three expressions often appear in forms such as *The first example is when he discovers...* or *The first chapter is where the protagonist discovers...* or *The reason is because he discovers...* But *when*, *where*, and *because* are subordinating conjunctions and are not meant to be written after the linking verb *is*. Here are some ways to revise. The first example occurs when he discovers... The first example is his discovery... The first chapter has the protagonist discovering... In the first chapter the protagonist discovers... The reason is that the protagonist discovers...
its	*Its* is a possessive pronoun. It is written without an apostrophe, like the possessive pronouns *yours*, *his*, *hers*, *ours*, and *theirs*. The puppy was lost but fortunately *its* name was on *its* collar.
it's	*It's* is the contraction for *it is* or *it has*. *It's* not necessary to use a calculator on this exam. *It's* been a very wet summer.
kind, sort, type	Use the singular *this* and *that* with the singular forms *kind*, *sort*, or *type*. Use the plural *these* and *those* with the plural forms *kinds*, *sorts*, or *types*. I have never understood *that kind* of word problem. She's had much experience with *these sorts* of issues. *Those types* of people are easy to make friends with.
lay	*Lay* means "to put or to place." It is a transitive verb and is used with a direct object. The principal parts are *lay, laid, laid, laying* The armies refused to *lay* down their weapons during the holiday. He *laid* his homework on the teacher's desk. I have never *laid* wall-to-wall carpeting before. She's been *laying* the newspapers in front of the wrong doors all week.
lie	*Lie* means "to recline" or "to be located." It is an intransitive verb and thus has no direct object. The principal parts are *lie, lay, lain, lying*. The doctor told me to *lie* down. Our base camp still *lay* a good four miles ahead of us. I should not have *lain* in the sun for that long. That dog has been *lying* in that position for over two hours. *Lie* may also mean "to speak falsely." It too is intransitive. Its principal parts are *lie, lied, lied, lying*. There was no need to *lie* about your age on the application. Not only did he steal the wallet, but then he *lied* about it. I have sometimes exaggerated, but I have never knowingly *lied*. She could tell by his rapid blinking that he was *lying*.

liable	*Liable* denotes responsibility and/or being in a position to experience an undesired situation or result.
	The money was missing from the register, and she held me *liable*. If you play with fire, you are *liable* to get hurt.
likely	*Likely* denotes probability. Before an infinitive, it implies a normal, customary, and therefore probable event.
	The weatherman said that rain was *likely* before midnight. If criticized, she is *likely* to break down and cry.
apt	*Apt* means "suitable" or "having a tendency." Before an infinitive, it too implies a customary event and may be interchanged with *likely*.
	They said I was an *apt* candidate for the Peace Corps. If criticized he is *apt* to break down and cry.
nauseated	*Nauseated* as an adjective means "feeling nausea; desiring to vomit."
	I feel *nauseated* at the sight of ketchup on scrambled eggs.
nauseous	Nauseous means "causing nausea." Use this word to describe things that make you feel nauseated.
	A *nauseous* odor from the chemistry lab filled the corridor.
no...or	You remember the correlative conjunctions *either...or* and *neither...nor*. When using the word *no*, use the conjunction *or*.
	There was *no* rhyme *or* reason for her behavior.
of	Do not write *of* with a verb when you should be using the helping verb *have*. This error occurs because a spoken expression such as *"could've"* sounds like *"could of."* A quick review of Chapter 1, "Verbs," will remind you of the correct forms of helping verbs.
off	*Off* is a preposition by itself and does not need to be followed by *of*.
	He laughed so hard he fell *off* his chair.
OK **O.K.** **okay**	All are acceptable spellings. Recognize, though, that the tone of the expression is usually considered casual, and a different word might be more suitable for formal writing.

principal	This word can be used as either a noun or an adjective. You have probably learned that the *principal* of the school is your *pal*. The principal is also the most important person in the school, and so as an adjective, the word means "most important, or chief." You have studied the *principal* parts of verbs. The word also means "a debt on which interest is calculated."
	Money, pure and simple, is my *principal* reason for that awful job. The interest is determined by the remaining *principal* on the loan.
principle	This word is used only as a noun. A principle is a "rule" or "fundamental truth." Notice that both *principle* and *rule* end with the letters *le*.
	She was a person of impeccable *principles*, discipline, and courage.

stationary	*Stationary* means "not moving" or "unchanging."
	Every day I spend thirty minutes on a *stationary* bicycle.
stationery	*Stationery* has to do with paper and other letter writing materials. Notice that *letter*, *paper*, and *stationery* all contain the letters *er*.
	We stocked up on supplies at the *stationery* store before school began.

there **their** **they're**	*There* is often some confusion about how these words are spelled. *Their* sounds are exactly the same. *They're* really quite easy if you pay attention.

USAGE

Name: _____

EXERCISE C: part two — usage editing   Accuracy _____

Directions: All of the sentences below contain at least one error in usage that was covered in Part Two. Draw a line through any word that is not used correctly, and put the correct form beneath it in the space provided.

Example: ~~Irregardless~~ of the price, those ~~kind~~ of brackets will never support this curtain.
Regardless   *kinds*

1. The reason he left school early is because he was feeling nauseous after he fell off of the swing.

    _____

2. The principal benefits of a stationery bicycle are it's low cost and portability.

    _____

3. In her remarks she inferred I was liable to win the election if I made less public appearances.

    _____

4. It is two miles further to take the trail that lies near the river, and you are apt to get lost.

    _____

5. They should have hung him while they had there chance.

    _____

6. There was hardly no peace nor quiet in the campground all night.

    _____

7. The biggest problem was when we all became nauseated from the experiment and it's vapors.

    _____

8. The principles of utopia imply that the possibility of perfection lays in all human hearts.

    _____

9. "I will discuss this no farther," said the principal; lay your spray cans down and leave."

    _____

10. Its these kind of people who are liable to get in trouble if there not careful.

    _____

USAGE

Name: _____

EXERCISE D: part two — usage writing   **Accuracy** _____ **Creativity** _____

Directions: The directions for this exercise are the same as for Exercise B.

1. (less; it's) _____

   _____

2. (nauseous; its) _____

   _____

3. (likely; imply) _____

   _____

4. (liable; principle) _____

   _____

5. (hardly; further) _____

   _____

6. (kind[s] of; infer) _____

   _____

7. (hanged; fewer) _____

   _____

8. (regardless; stationery) _____

   _____

9. (they're; hung) _____

   _____

10. (lay; reason…is…that) _____

    _____

11. (nauseated; scarcely) _____

_____

12. (no...or; stationary) _____

_____

13. (example occurs when; their) _____

_____

14. (okay; lie [recline] in past tense) _____

_____

15. (there; implicit) _____

_____

16. (farther; principle) _____

_____

17. (off; apt) _____

_____

18. (principal; type of) _____

_____

19. (lie [speak falsely]; hardly) _____

_____

20. (reason...is...that; further) _____

_____

11. PUNCTUATION

The uses of punctuation fall into two categories, **conventional** and **stylistic**. We put periods at the ends of sentences, question marks after questions, commas between items in a series, all because they are the conventional thing to do. It does not matter what that sentence says, what that question asks, or what the items in the series are. Stylistic punctuation, on the other hand, is much more the result of a writer's style, as well as of the actual content of the material. Sometimes authors want to whisper, so they use parentheses; sometimes the adjective clause is essential, and there are no commas, and sometimes it is nonessential, so there are. How authors punctuate their writing can have a dramatic effect on the reader. Review Edgar Allan Poe's "The Tell-Tale Heart" for a wonderful lesson in stylistic punctuation.

As you worked your way through this book, you probably noticed several interesting ways that punctuation was being used in the exercises. Now that you are thoroughly familiar with all the grammar terminology, the punctuation rules will make sense. And, with practice, you will gain confidence in using those grammatical constructions, and punctuating them correctly, to achieve your own personal writing style.

CONVENTIONAL PUNCTUATION

Period

At the end of a sentence	Punctuation is very important. My feet hurt. I'll be home by 10:00 p.m.
After a mild command	Take out the trash. Erase any stray marks on your paper.
After an abbreviation	Feb. Mr. Mrs. Dr. Ave. a.m. St. etc. et al. Jr.
Exceptions—postal codes, dates, organizations, common terms	TX NY CBS FBI MLK USMC UCLA AD NBA BC

Exclamation Mark

After an exclamation	My, what big teeth you have! What a fantastic view!
After a strong command	Get out of my sight! Stop!

Question Mark

After a question	Will you marry me? Did any of my friends call?
After a question within a statement	My question is, How did the fight begin? "Why is the sky blue?" asks the child.

Comma

Between items in a series	Under the seat cushion she found potato chips, a comb, two pencils, and a dime.

Note: If one or more of the items contains the word *and,* write the series in an order that avoids confusion. Also, you should always put a comma before the final *and.*

His walls were lined with photographs of such famous comedians as W. C. Fields, the Marx Brothers, Laurel and Hardy, and Charlie Chaplin.

Between adjectives before a noun	I found a hungry, wet, abandoned kitten.
Compare:	I found a hungry, wet Irish Setter.
Two independent clauses joined by a coordinating conjunction	We tried to convince her to go with us, but she said she had work to do.
After certain introductory words	Oh, Yes, No, Why, Well,
To set off a noun of direct address	Jane, are you sure of that? Do you know, sir, when the next train leaves? I'm sorry I broke the window, Mrs. Davis.
To set off parenthetical expressions and interjections *on the contrary, by the way, on the other hand, of course, indeed, for example,* etc.	By the way, your favorite store is having a sale. Most people, of course, don't even bother. It was just a wrong number, after all. Jeepers, I never expected she would return my call.
Items in dates or addresses	On Friday, November 22, 1963, President Kennedy was assassinated. Springfield, Massachusetts, is the home of the Basketball Hall of Fame.
Note: the comma is omitted if no day is given or if the day precedes the name of the month	January 1947 was our coldest January on record. You have until 15 February to submit your proposal.
Between a name and a title (Jr., Ph.D., M.D.), and after that title if the sentence continues	Harold Jones, Jr., M.D., has his office at Beth Israel Hospital.
After the salutation of a friendly letter, and after the closing of any letter	Dear Dad, Dear Aunt Doris, Sincerely yours, Respectfully,
To avoid misreading	If you can, come to our party. Below, the engine room was filled with water.

Semicolon

Between items in a series if one or more of the items contain a comma	At the head of the table sat Henry; the President, Mr. Ogden; the Founder, Mrs. Morgan; Henry's grandmother; and yours truly.

Apostrophe

With the letter *s,* to form the possessive of a singular noun or indefinite pronoun	dog's collar James's balloon everyone's name
Note: If the singular noun is more than one syllable and ends in *s*, the additional *s* is sometimes omitted.	Jesus' name Xerxes' ship Odysseus' son
To form the possessive of a plural noun ending in *s*	houses' windows computers' usefulness
With *s,* to form the possessive of a plural noun not ending in *s*	children's toys mice's nest

Note: All the possessives end in both an apostrophe and an *s*, either in the order 's or s'.

In certain time and money expressions	a day's wait one dollar's worth	four years' work five dollars' worth
In contractions	doesn't let's	can't it's
To form plurals of lowercase letters, and abbreviations	three *a*'s	*p*'s and *q*'s
Note: The apostrophe is optional in plurals where there is no confusion.	three *B*'s three *B*s	the 1960's two *4*'s the 1960s two *4*s

Italics (Underlining)

Titles of books, magazines, works of art, movies, ships, etc.	the *Boston Globe* *Mona Lisa*	*Crazy Rich Asians* *Spirit of St. Louis*
Foreign words	*bon appetit*	*wunderbar*
Words, letters, numbers, and symbols when referred to as such	The letter *p* is silent in the word *pneumonia*. Your *7* looks like a *1*. Don't write @ when you mean *at*. Having two *A*'s and three *B*'s puts you on the honor roll.	

Quotation Marks

To enclose a direct quotation	"You may come in now," said the doctor. My mother told me, "Wear your hat." "You know," she said, "he'd like to meet you."

Note: If the quoted material is part of the main sentence, do not set it off with commas.

He told us to "fish or cut bait."

Note: The comma or period always goes inside the closing quotation marks. A question mark or exclamation mark goes inside the closing quotation marks if the quote is itself a question or an exclamation. Otherwise, it goes outside.

Did you ask, "How's the weather?"
Did you say, "Good morning"?
She yelled, "Fire!"
Did she yell, "Fire!"? (rare)

To enclose titles of short stories, poems, magazine and newspaper articles, songs, chapters, and other short writings.

"To Build a Fire."
"Where Have All the Flowers Gone?"
"The Dover Road"

Note: Use a single quotation mark (apostrophe) to enclose quoted material within a quotation.

She asked, "Have you read 'Mending Wall,' by Robert Frost?"

To enclose slang or ironic words or phrases, or to define another word or phrase

What did he mean when he said it was "rad"?
Has your "contribution" to the government gone up this year? (slang for taxes)
Stationary means "not moving."

Colon

In expressions of time, in Bible references, and after the salutation of a business letter	The train leaves at 12:47 a.m. Do you know what John 3:16 says? Dear Mrs. Henderson: Gentlemen:
To indicate "note what follows"	Here's the plan: we all clean out the garage, then Mom will drive us to the movies.

Hyphen

To split a word at the end of a typed line	I just received a letter containing a wonderful invitation.
With the prefixes *self-* and *all-*; with the suffix *-elect*; with all prefixes before a proper noun or a proper adjective	self-centered all-star congresswoman-elect pre-Columbian non-Asian
For compound numbers from twenty-one to ninety-nine; with fractions and compound adjectives when written before the noun they modify (except with an *-ly* adverb)	seventy-six two hundred and thirty-six a two-thirds majority three-year-old child half-eaten sandwich well-written paper Your paper was well written. This is a poorly written paper.

PUNCTUATION

Name: _____

EXERCISE A: conventional punctuation   Accuracy: _____ Creativity _____

Directions: Fill in the blank spaces with your own creations, punctuated correctly. Also put the appropriate punctuation at the end of the sentence, and elsewhere as needed.

1. On _____ _____
    (month, day, year)   *(scientist's name)*

    will launch his rocket, _____ , toward the moon
    (rocket's name)

2. _____ first short story, _____ ,
    (name of person, possessive)   *(story title)*

    will be published in _____
    (magazine title)

3. The fact that Mr _____ son is named _____ Jr
    (name of person, possessive)   *(name of son)*

    causes occasional confusion

4. Up in Grandpas attic we found _____
    (items in a series, with commas and semicolons)

    _____

5. _____ asked the professor
    (beginning of quotation)

    _____
    (end of quotation – include a book title)

6. Does the word _____ have two _____ or one?
    (spelling word)   *(letters)*

7. Most _____ _____
    (plural noun, possessive)   *(plural noun)*

    _____ are _____
    (parenthetical expression)   *(adjective)*

    _____ _____
    (adjective)   *(plural noun)*

8. _____ _____
    (introductory element)   *(noun of direct address)*

    _____ never read _____
    (contraction)   *(book or magazine title)*

9. _____
    (quotation ending with short story title)

    _____ he inquired

EXERCISE B: reading for conventional punctuation   Accuracy: _____

Directions: Now read and try to find examples of conventional punctuation. Your best bets for the most examples are either a popular magazine or a history or social studies textbook with lots of facts. Fill in the spaces below with your samples as indicated. You do not have to copy the full sentence, just enough to illustrate the punctuation and provide some context. Also tell the source or sources you used. You may not find them all, but collect as many as you can in a reasonable amount of time.

_____   _____
(hyphen for compound noun or adjective)   *(commas in date or address)*

_____   _____
(apostrophe in a contraction)   *(apostrophe in possessive of singular noun)*

_____   _____
(apostrophe in possessive of plural noun)   *(italics for book or magazine title)*

_____   _____
(comma after certain introductory words)   *(parenthetical expression)*

_____   _____
(quotation marks for short story, poem, etc.)   *(period after an abbreviation)*

_____
(question mark inside quotes)

_____
(commas between items in a series)

_____
(commas between adjectives before a noun)

_____
(comma before a direct quote)

_____
(comma at the end of a direct quote)

_____
(semicolons with items in a series that also contain commas)

_____
(colon to indicate "note what follows")

Sources: _____   _____

_____   _____

STYLISTIC PUNCTUATION

Comma

After any introductory participial phrase, infinitive phrase, or adverb clause:

Hoping to catch a glimpse of the movie star, we stood on the front bumper of our car.

Discouraged by the results of the primary, the candidate withdrew from the race.

To better their chances in the job market, they took a course in word processing.

If I ever get to Australia, I'm definitely going to climb Ayer's Rock.

After two or more introductory prepositional phrases:

With a glance over his shoulder to the runner on first, the pitcher began his wind-up.

On the top shelf in the closet, Mother piled her out-of-fashion shoes.

Within or at the end of a sentence, to set off nonessential phrases or clauses:

A bit of explanation is necessary at this point. This comma rule applies to modifiers: participial phrases, infinitive phrases, prepositional phrases, appositive phrases, and adjective clauses.

Sometimes these modifiers are essential to our understanding of the words being modified, and sometimes they only add interesting but nonessential information. Some grammar books call them "restrictive" and "nonrestrictive" modifiers.

Generally the modifier is nonessential if we are telling about a proper noun, or if the modifier applies to that one noun only or to all such nouns, or if we are expressing common knowledge. Such modifiers will be set off from the main clause with commas.

Ms. Thibideau, the school band leader, is organizing a band trip to Germany.

The girl scouts, on their first overnight camping trip, kept their leaders hopping.

Shakespeare's last play, *The Tempest,* was written in 1611.

The members of the Spirit Committee, who are elected annually, met the treasurer.

Egbert, hearing his name read over the radio, nearly drove off the road.

But if the modifier applies to one or only some of the nouns and not to all of them, or if we are expressing limited, not common, knowledge, then we must not use commas. The modifier is presenting essential information and must not be set apart from the main sentence.

Any dog needing a rabies shot can get one at Saturday's clinic.

She wanted to get the window broken by the tree branch repaired before dark.

Shakespeare's play *The Merchant of Venice* opens with Antonio's "sadness" speech.

Seniors who have a *B+* average or better do not have to take the final exam.

Her two friends riding in the back seat kept distracting her from her driving lesson.

To set off an absolute phrase in any position in the sentence (see also Chapter 8):

With our fang-like teeth firmly in place and our masks lowered, we rang the doorbell.

The stand-up comic, her upper lip sweating in the spotlight, was quickly losing the audience.

The gymnast hung from the rings, his arms extended in a perfect "iron cross."

Between phrases and clauses in a series:

We know how to use commas with items in a series. We can also "stack" any of the phrases and clauses that we studied and thus generate some very interesting and powerful sentences.

present participial phrases	All afternoon we relaxed, lying by the pool, playing bocce on the lawn, and listening to oldies on the radio.
infinitives	Ulysses encouraged his men "to strive, to seek, to find, and not to yield."
prepositional phrases	The dog will have to go either into the basement, out in the back yard, or on her line.
noun clauses	Today we must discuss when we should schedule the semiformal, where we should have it, and who will be in charge.

Semicolon

Between two independent clauses not joined by a coordinating conjunction.

We knew there would be a crowd at the ball park; admission was free.

Between two independent clauses joined by a coordinating conjunction, if there are other commas in the sentence that might cause confusion:

The make-your-own-sundae table offered many flavors, including pistachio and cookies and cream; but no vanilla was to be seen anywhere.

Colon

Before a long, formal statement or quotation; to introduce a formal list or an explanation or elaboration of what has already been said:

Note: When used in this way, the colon must be preceded by a full sentence, one containing either a direct object or the words *as follows* or *the following*.

The graduation speaker made her final point: Don't forget to thank the loan officer!

Dash

Before an explanation to imply "in other words"; to indicate an abrupt break in thought; after an introductory series:

I know of only one way to keep my car from being stolen—sell it.

The trouble started—it was all Gina's idea—when we found the box of matches.

Screwdrivers, wrenches, hammer—all were lying in a puddle of rusty water.

Parentheses

To set off supplementary ideas, explanations, or "whispered" asides:

The map (see page 17) shows the old boundary between East and West Germany.

The mayor (according to one source) will not run for re-election this fall.

He stood at the bottom of the stairs (could this be the night?) holding a bouquet of roses.

PUNCTUATION

Name: _____

EXERCISE C: stylistic punctuation

Accuracy: _____ Creativity _____

Directions: Fill in the blank spaces with sentences of your own creation, according to the punctuation and directions given. Notice the punctuation marks over on the right side of the line.

1. _____ ;

   (independent clause)

   _____ .

   (independent clause)

2. _____ :

   (explanation or elaboration)

   _____ .

3. _____ (_____)

   (whispered aside)

   _____ .

4. _____ — _____

   (abrupt break)

   _____ — _____ .

5. _____ ,

   (absolute phrase)

   _____ .

6. _____ , _____ ,

   (adjective clause)

   _____ .

7. _____ , _____

   (two prepositional phrases)

   _____ .

8. _____ , _____

   (infinitive phrase)

   _____ .

9. _____ ; _____ ,

   (conjunctive adverb)

   _____ .

10. _____ ,

    (independent clause)

    _____ , _____

    (past participial phrase)   *(past participial phrase)*

    _____ , and _____ .

    (present participial phrase)

PUNCTUATION

EXERCISE D: reading for stylistic punctuation   **Accuracy:** _____

Directions: Now read and try to find examples of stylistic punctuation. Your best bets for the most examples are either a challenging magazine or a sophisticated novel. Fill in the spaces below with your samples as indicated. You do not have to copy the full sentence, just enough to illustrate the punctuation and provide some context. Also tell the source or sources you used. You may not find them all, but collect as many as you can in a reasonable amount of time.

_____
(comma after an introductory participial phrase)

_____
(comma after an introductory adverb clause)

_____
(commas to set off a nonessential adjective clause)

_____
(comma to set off an absolute phrase)

_____
(comma after two or more introductory prepositional phrases)

_____
(commas to set off a nonessential appositive)

_____
(comma to set off a participial phrase at the end of the sentence)

_____
(semicolon between independent clauses without a conjunction)

_____
(semicolon between independent clauses with a conjunctive adverb)

_____
(colon before a formal statement or explanation)

_____
(dash for any reason)

_____
(parentheses for any reason)

Sources: _____

12. WRITING PATTERNS

Now that you have learned the pieces of the writing puzzle—parts of the sentence, parts of speech, phrases, clauses, and punctuation—it is time to put them all together. We will use two new terms to describe how a sentence is constructed.

Base clause: A base clause is a sentence, with a subject, a predicate, and maybe a few adjectives, adverbs, and prepositional phrases along the way. It is the central grammatical unit, to which we will add free modifiers, as discussed in the next section.

We label a base clause by putting the number 1 at the beginning of it. Sometimes we refer to the base clause as a **Level 1**.

Free modifier: A free modifier is any word, phrase, or clause that is set apart from the base clause by some form of punctuation. It is called *free* because of its separateness from the base clause, and also because free modifiers (except for the adjective clause) are often free to move around in a sentence and appear in more than one location. We will label a free modifier as a **Level 2**, **Level 3**, and so on, depending on what it modifies. A Level 2 will modify something in the Level 1, a Level 3 will modify something in the Level 2. Together these form **Levels of Generality.** The Level 1 serves as the foundation, and each additional level further describes, explains, compares, or otherwise clarifies the idea expressed in the previous level.

Here are some examples that show how these levels of generality work together. You should be able to identify the grammatical structure of each free modifier.

- 1 He got back up quickly,
  - 2 blinking in the darkness,
  - 2 his mouth warm with blood.—Michael Crichton, *Jurassic Park*

- 1 I pedal furiously now,
  - 2 not because I want to catch up with them,
  - 2 but because this road is deserted and I want to reach a better road or highway as soon as possible.—Robert Cormier, *I Am the Cheese*

- 1 Sophie knelt up,
  - 2 her hands covered in earth,
  - 2 her hair awry, and
  - 2 an expression on her face that Penelope had never seen before.
    —Rosamunde Pilcher, *The Shell Seekers*

- 1 He is a poorly educated man,
  - 2 small,
  - 2 active,
  - 2 with his right leg off, and
  - 2 wearing a wooden stump which is worn away upon the inner side.
    —Sir Arthur Conan Doyle, "The Sign of the Four"

- 1 Cordelia sits with nonchalance,
  - 2 nudging me with her elbow now and then,
  - 2 staring blankly at the other people with her gray-green eyes,
    - 3 opaque and glinting as metal.—Margaret Atwood, *Cat's Eye*

- 1 Harriet Blacking was the dark presence in the school,
  - 2 a rather small girl,
    - 3 plump,
    - 3 nearly neckless,
    - 3 with dead-white skin and the thinnest nose Catherine had ever seen,
      - 4 as thin as the blade of a pocketknife.
        —Paula Fox, *The Moonlight Man*

If a free modifier is located within the base clause or another free modifier, we use the symbol / to show that there has been an interruption. We also label the interrupter with a / symbol after the level number. Here are some examples.

- 1 We went up the riverbank, / , and threaded our way through a labyrinth of silver-grey boulders and rust-red anthills,
  - 2/ falling into single file again
  - 2 shaped variously like witches caps or the figures of kneeling giants or like trees without branches.—Beryl Markham, *West with the Night*

- 2 As he drew closer to the cry,
- 1 he went more slowly,
  - 2 with caution in every movement,
  - 2 till he came to an open place among the trees, and looking out saw, / , a long, lean, timber wolf.
    - 3/ erect on haunches
    - 3/ with nose pointed to the sky—Jack London, *The Call of the Wild*

Here is a summary of the most common free modifiers.

1. adjectives
2. adverbs
3. prepositional phrases (often with *like)*
4. appositive
5. present participial phrase
6. past participial phrase
7. infinitive phrase
8. adjective clause
9. adverb clause
10. absolute phrase

In Exercise A, be able to identify what each modifier is. In later exercises you will be asked to fill in your own free modifiers.

WRITING PATTERNS

Name: _____

EXERCISE A: levels of generality   **Accuracy:** _____

Directions: Lay out the following sentences by the numbers, as shown on the previous two pages, to indicate the "Levels of Generality," indenting where necessary. There may be more blank lines for you to write on than there are levels, since some levels may need more than one line to write out. Do not include the title and author.

1. Portia, waiting for Eddie as she had often waited, turned her fists round slowly in her pockets, regretting that he should have been called away just now. —Elizabeth Bowen, *The Death of the Heart*

    _____

    _____

    _____

2. I've been walking for hours it seems, down the hill to the downtown, where the streetcars no longer run. —Margaret Atwood, *Cat's Eye*

    _____

    _____

3. The captain soon knuckled under, put up his weapon, and resumed his seat, grumbling like a beaten dog. —Robert Louis Stevenson, *Treasure Island*

    _____

    _____

4. Just as Mr. Summers left off talking and turned to the assembled villagers, Mrs. Hutchinson came hurriedly along the path to the square, her sweater thrown over her shoulder, and slid into place at the back of the crowd. —Shirley Jackson, "The Lottery"

    _____

    _____

    _____

5. Ralph stood now, one hand against an enormous red block, a block large as a mill wheel that had been split off and hung, tottering. —William Golding, *Lord of the Flies*

    _____

    _____

    _____

    _____

6. After a little while Mr. Gatz opened the door and came out, his mouth ajar, his face flushed lightly, his eyes leaking isolated and unpunctual tears. — F. Scott Fitzgerald, *The Great Gatsby*

_____

_____

_____

_____

7. It was nearly nine o'clock when Squealer made his appearance, walking slowly and dejectedly, his eyes dull, his tail hanging limply behind him, and with every appearance of being seriously ill. — George Orwell, *Animal Farm*

_____

_____

_____

_____

_____

8. Ursula's blanket — or, rather Julian's old army blanket — was folded, palletlike, in the corner of the hut, just as it had been when I first surprised her lying on it, trying to read her book. — Gail Godwin, *The Finishing School*

_____

_____

_____

_____

_____

9. He stood patiently in front of her, as he had stood in front of the lieutenant, listening. — Graham Greene, *The Power and the Glory*

_____

_____

_____

10. Deborah had looked about and found that she could not see except in outlines, gray against gray, and with no depth, but flatly, like a picture. — Hannah Green, *I Never Promised You a Rose Garden*

_____

_____

_____

_____

WRITING PATTERNS

Name: _____

EXERCISE B: writing levels of generality

Accuracy: _____ Creativity: _____

Directions: In the following sentences, we have provided the base clause. Fill in the other levels with free modifiers as suggested. Be alert to where each sentence ends and the next begins.

1.   2 _____ ,

         (present participial phrase)

   1 he cautiously entered the cave,

    2 _____ .

         (comparison)

2. 1 She sat on the edge of the swimming pool,

    2 _____ ,

         (present participial phrase)

     3 _____ .

         (adverb clause)

3. 1 The patient, / , seemed well on the road to recovery.

    2/ _____ but

         (past participial phrase)

    2/ _____

         (present participial phrase)

4.   2 _____ ,

         (infinitive phrase as adverb, telling why)

     3 _____ ,

         (adjective clause)

   1 our neighbors built an eight-foot stockade fence around their whole property.

5. 1 The new champion stood proudly on the pedestal,

    2 _____ and

         (absolute phrase)

    2 _____ .

         (absolute phrase)

6.   2 _____ ,

         (adverb clause)

   1 the rescue party fanned out in all directions,

    2 _____ .

         (present participial phrase)

7. 1 One by one the marathon runners, / , crossed the finish line.

    2/ _____ but _____
          (adjective)   *(adjective)*

8. 2 _____ and _____ ,
          (adverb)   *(adverb)*

    3 _____ ,
                              (comparison)

    1 he unscrewed the cap.

9. 1 She browsed through the Travel Section of the Sunday newspaper,

    2 _____ ,
                         (present participial phrase)

    3 _____ .
                              (appositive)

10. 1 I'm running out of time to finish my project,

    2 _____ ,
                              (appositive)

    2 _____ .
                            (adverb clause)

11. 2 _____ ,
                         (present participial phrase)

    1 the ambassador extended her hand toward the consul,

    2 _____ .
                            (adjective clause)

12. 1 They told us to form two lines,

    2 _____ and
                              (appositive)

    2 _____ .
                              (appositive)

13. 1 I sat quietly in the waiting room,

    2 _____ ,
                         (present participial phrase)

    3 _____ ,
                            (adjective clause)

    4 _____ .
                            (adverb clause)

14.   2 _____ ,
                 (simple adverb)

       2 _____ , and
                 (past participial phrase)

       2 _____ ,
                 (present participial phrase)

    1 they rounded the turn and headed for home.

15.   2 With _____ ,
                 (absolute phrase)

    1 the doctor came out of the operating room,

       2 _____ .
                 (present participial phrase)

16. 1 The magnificent Bengal tiger roamed through its realistic habitat,

       2 _____ ,
                 (present participial phrase)

       2 _____ ,
                 (present participial phrase)

         3 _____ .
                    (adverb clause)

17. 1 Most of the fans have been standing in line for over two hours,

       2 _____ ,
                 (absolute phrase)

       2 _____ .
                 (absolute phrase)

18. 1 Mr. and Mrs. Killian, / , were honored at the annual dinner last night.

      2/ _____ and
                 (appositive)

      2/ _____
                 (appositive)

19. 1 The athletic fields, / , were ready for the first game of the season.

      2/ _____ and
                 (past participial phrase)

      2/ _____
                 (past participial phrase)

20.   2 _____ ,

                (infinitive phrase as adverb, telling why)

        3 _____ ,

                (adjective clause)

    1 the School Committee met far into the night.

21.   1 The baby loved the new toy,

      2 _____ ,

                (appositive)

        3 _____ ,

                (past participial phrase)

           4 _____ .

                    (comparison)

22.   2 _____ ,

                (appositive)

      2 _____ ,

                (appositive)

      2 _____

                (appositive)

    1 —everything was finally packed for our cross-country camping trip.

23.   2 _____ and

                (past participial phrase)

      2 _____ ,

                (present participial phrase)

    1 the puppy looked mournfully up at me,

      2 _____ .

                (present participial phrase)

24.   2 _____ ,

                (adverb clause)

        3 _____ ,

                (adjective clause)

    1 the florist trimmed off the dead leaves and snipped the bottoms of the stems.

25.   1 The sprinter settled into the starting blocks,

      2 _____ ,

                (adverb clause)

      2 _____ .

                (adverb clause)

13. THE IDEA BANK

Welcome to the **Idea Bank**. Here you will find an impressive collection of nouns, adjectives, and adverbs just waiting to squeeze themselves into your writing or to inspire similar creations from your own imagination. Before we begin, though, here are a few tips you might find helpful.

- You can get double duty from the present participles through a simple variation. Just change the verb to the past participle form and put the word *having* in front of it. Thus, *waiting in the doctor's office* becomes *having waited in the doctor's office* and *sitting alone on the subway* becomes *having sat alone on the subway*.

- You may also stretch the infinitive phrases used as nouns by adding *how, where, when,* or *why* at the beginning of the phrase. Thus, *I wanted to get the work done* becomes *I knew where to get the work done* and *I tried to glue the model plane together* becomes *He asked how to glue the model plane together*.

- Make sure when you are using the *-ing* phrases that you are using them correctly, as adjectives or as nouns.

  Pouring a glass of milk, the waiter suddenly sneezed.   **adjective**
  Pouring a glass of milk was not as easy as it looked.   **noun**

- Make sure when you are using the past participles that they are adjectives and not main verbs.

  The rope had been *attached at both ends*.   **main verb**
  The rope, *attached at both ends*, presented a challenge.   **adjective**

Now let's get a little silly and have some fun. Here are a few suggestions about how you and your friends can grab some ideas from the Idea Bank and make up some pretty unusual sentences. Enjoy!

- Write down a subject and a verb, and maybe a direct object, indirect object, predicate nominative, or predicate adjective. Then, randomly select items from the Idea Bank and add them to your sentence. You might end up with sentences like *As if he were a railroad engineer, my cat, which had kept us so warm all these years, purred to hear the music better* or *Watching the eighth-grade play, nobody knew whether the job would ever be finished*.

- Toss open a dictionary and read out the first noun you see. Modify it with a randomly selected participial phrase. Imagine *the king taking advantage of the situation* and *the auditorium that I was expecting*.

- Make up your own Idea Bank items, and share them with your friends. Just brainstorm. Or, take phrases and clauses from books you have enjoyed reading.

- Get several of your friends together and each take a part of the sentence to write. Write the parts separately, then read them all together.

- Create compounds by selecting more than one unit from each Idea Bank category. You might end up with *Going at top speed and taking advantage of the situation, we tried to take out the trash and to fit everything into the trunk.*

- Watch television or listen to Public Radio and write down new Idea Bank items that you hear. Compare "the soaps," the situation comedies, the dramas, the news. Write a minute's worth of script for the show of your choice.

- Select a book you enjoyed reading in your younger years. Does it use modifiers like these? If so, add some of them to your Idea Bank inventory. If not, could you add some of your own to the story? Would they make the story better?

- Make up some nonsense items and see if your friends can identify what they are. For example, what sort of grammatical construction is each of these?

  gazorbing on the flubby biddle
  to jempag a rottynorg clastel
  although higdorf couldn't tambo the wassemvit
  florged by the quescent

- Try combining Idea Bank items with coordinating or correlative conjunctions. This could lead to *smelling like a rose but behaving like a wild monkey* or *not only considered a leader in her field but also chosen by vote of the faculty.*

- Now, let yourself go and try to write a huge sentence—full of modifiers, conjunctions, phrases and clauses. Is length all that bad? All that good? Can you find a place for it in your writing?

- Look for opportunities to use these grammatical structures and sentence patterns in your other writing assignments besides creative writing. Could you use a conjunctive adverb such as *consequently* or *nevertheless* between independent clauses in a science report? In your essay for English class, could you use a series of infinitive phrases to explain a character's actions? Would an introductory participial phrase help explain an army's tactics in a history paper? Look closely at your textbooks, in newspaper editorials, and in good nonfiction writing everywhere, to see how professional writers use these patterns.

present participial phrases (adjectives) *or* gerund phrases (nouns)

1. sitting alone on the subway
2. pouring a glass of milk
3. filling out the insurance form
4. finishing the night's assignment
5. putting on the finishing touches
6. stepping up to home plate
7. taking out the library book
8. pushing the shopping cart
9. wondering about the future
10. knowing that she would be late
11. going about his business
12. skating the length of the rink
13. opening the cereal box
14. being the first in line
15. smelling like a rose
16. turning into a werewolf
17. figuring out the best way
18. asking for a raise
19. snorkeling in the Florida Keys
20. fixing the leaking roof
21. trying to tie her shoelace
22. rolling out of bed
23. writing in my diary
24. selling his baseball cards
25. turning her jacket inside out
26. waiting in the doctor's office
27. behaving like a wild monkey
28. watching the eighth-grade play
29. measuring the pancake mix
30. signing her name in the guestbook
31. renovating old houses
32. failing to find any evidence
33. staying in the nicest hotel
34. rotting under the back deck
35. talking for hours on the telephone
36. cleaning up after the party
37. striving to make the honor roll
38. going at top speed
39. wallpapering the bathroom
40. taking care of the children
41. shampooing the dog
42. finding a spider in his sleeping bag
43. mowing the lawn
44. letting their imaginations run wild
45. taking advantage of the situation
46. cutting the coupons from the paper
47. growing old together
48. looking like a scarecrow
49. preparing to move to the country
50. dividing the money they had earned

past participial phrases (adjectives)

1.	attached at both ends	26.	named captain of the swim team
2.	burnt to a crisp	27.	pleased with her performance
3.	spilled from the cup	28.	woven from the finest silk
4.	nailed to the floor	29.	painted by an Australian aborigine
5.	left over from the party	30.	engaged to be married
6.	broken into a million pieces	31.	taken prisoner during the war
7.	elected to the city council	32.	stuck on the bottom of his shoe
8.	given a helping hand	33.	promised a reprieve by the governor
9.	located by the metal detector	34.	abandoned on the front doorstep
10.	found cheating on the exam	35.	awarded first prize in the contest
11.	considered a leader in her field	36.	sought for burglary and arson
12.	driven by a novice	37.	sent an invitation to the wedding
13.	honored at the banquet	38.	torn on a loose nail
14.	examined for termites	39.	learned by heart
15.	chosen by vote of the faculty	40.	honed to a sharp edge
16.	hung up in the back hall	41.	wrapped in a Navajo blanket
17.	destined to succeed	42.	determined to finish before dinner
18.	dyed a bright red	43.	damaged by the hurricane
19.	lost on the ski trip	44.	covered with sawdust
20.	soaked by the downpour	45.	scolded for hitting his little brother
21.	made from old tin cans	46.	born to be a leader
22.	infected from the scratch	47.	overturned in the marketplace
23.	stalled in traffic	48.	frightened by the wailing sound
24.	stapled to the bill	49.	promised a raise by his boss
25.	shot by the hunter	50.	photographed from 30,000 feet

infinitive phrases (adjectives, adverbs, or nouns)

1.	to get the work done	26.	to decide on a name for your pet
2.	to depend on your friends	27.	to spend the holiday at the beach
3.	to be seen and enjoyed	28.	to distinguish one from the other
4.	to ask for directions	29.	to glue the model plane together
5.	to rebuild the cathedral	30.	to be staged by an interior decorator
6.	to replace the joystick	31.	to dry-clean my suede jacket
7.	to hear the music better	32.	to subscribe to any magazines
8.	to tie a string around my finger	33.	to allow her to do that
9.	to put it in your suitcase	34.	to take out the trash
10.	to do my summer reading	35.	to raise money for the charity
11.	to wake up first	36.	to climb to the top of the mountain
12.	to work backstage	37.	to return the overdue library books
13.	to stay in a hotel	38.	to talk with your mouth full
14.	to renew the dog's license	39.	to bite off more than he can chew
15.	to be afraid of the dark	40.	to achieve your goals in life
16.	to practice what you preach	41.	to pretend you are a vampire
17.	to keep the old car running	42.	to see your story in print
18.	to fit everything into the trunk	43.	to settle down and get to work
19.	to buy a new one	44.	to score the winning goal
20.	to win the lottery	45.	to recognize your obligation
21.	to finish before the bell rings	46.	to defend the principle of free speech
22.	to find a job for the summer	47.	to consider others first
23.	to have loved and lost	48.	to be late for dinner
24.	to act your age	49.	to give as a birthday gift
25.	to fill up the tank with gas	50.	to keep an open mind

noun clauses

1.	whether the job would ever be finished	17.	where he had hidden the jewels
2.	that we never should have sold it	18.	that none of the roses had bloomed
3.	what she meant by that remark	19.	what all the commotion was about
4.	where we could have our picnic	20	whichever runner gets to the bridge first
5.	why he couldn't find the other shoe		
6.	that everyone gets angry sometimes		
7.	whoever finds the buried treasure		
8.	the fact that the moon goes through phases		
9.	which airline we should take to Europe		
10.	when the package would arrive		
11.	whether he should ask her for the assignment		
12.	how I should start my term paper		
13.	who would be the best choice		
14.	whose answer was the right one		
15.	that neither choice would be inexpensive		
16.	why they never return my telephone calls		

adjective clauses

1. that had to be done
2. in which I grew up
3. which had kept us so warm all these years
4. that was empty
5. whose guess is closest to the actual amount
6. that had patches on the elbows
7. who raised two children by himself
8. from whom she received a wonderful recommendation
9. that I was expecting
10. whose ankle had been broken when the horse fell
11. that no one could ever believe
12. which wouldn't be finished for another two weeks
13. to whom the mayor presented the key to the city
14. who kicked the ball right over the goalie's head
15. which we found under the Christmas tree
16. whom everyone admired for his courage
17. which simply broke off in my hand
18. that didn't make any difference
19. whose fingerprints did not match those on the glass
20. with whom she will be going to the restaurant

adverb clauses

1. although I didn't really mean it
2. provided that you practice your cello first
3. lest we forget
4. until it is time for you to go
5. as if he were a railroad engineer
6. in order that we be fair to all concerned parties
7. if I can get my hands on one
8. before he even closed the door
9. so that she wouldn't have to get up again
10. unless the green one fits you better
11. though neither method will be easy
12. since we've already gone this far
13. than we had ever imagined
14. while the cakes are baking
15. whether you help me or not
16. till all the tickets are sold
17. wherever you can find a place for them
18. whereas only six people showed up for the tryouts
19. after all is said and done
20. as though I were never going to see her again

CPSIA information can be obtained
at www.ICGtesting.com
Printed in the USA
LVHW011500010922
727308LV00008B/516